Resource report for the deep-water areas of proposed OCS lease sale No. 70, St. George Basin, Alaska: USGS Open-File Report 80-246

et al., Alan K. Cooper, D. W. Scholl

The BiblioGov Project is an effort to expand awareness of the public documents and records of the U.S. Government via print publications. In broadening the public understanding of government and its work, an enlightened democracy can grow and prosper. Ranging from historic Congressional Bills to the most recent Budget of the United States Government, the BiblioGov Project spans a wealth of government information. These works are now made available through an environmentally friendly, print-on-demand basis, using only what is necessary to meet the required demands of an interested public. We invite you to learn of the records of the U.S. Government, heightening the knowledge and debate that can lead from such publications.

Included are the following Collections:

Budget of The United States Government
Presidential Documents
United States Code
Education Reports from ERIC
GAO Reports
History of Bills
House Rules and Manual
Public and Private Laws

Code of Federal Regulations
Congressional Documents
Economic Indicators
Federal Register
Government Manuals
House Journal
Privacy act Issuances
Statutes at Large

UNITED STATES DEPARTMENT OF THE INTERIOR
GEOLOGICAL SURVEY

RESOURCE REPORT FOR THE DEEP-WATER AREAS OF PROPOSED
OCS LEASE SALE NO. 70, ST. GEORGE BASIN, ALASKA

by

A. K. Cooper, D. W. Scholl, T. L. Vallier,
and E. W. Scott

Open File Report 80-246

This report is preliminary and
has not been edited or reviewed
for conformity with Geological
Survey standards and nomenclature.

Menlo Park, California
October, 1979

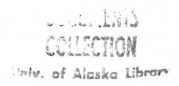

TABLE OF CONTENTS

SUMMARY

The St. George Basin lease area #70 has been divided into two parts: a shallow-water shelf area that is described by Marlow and others (1979a) and a deep-water slope and rise area that is described in this report. This deep-water area is herein named the Umnak Plateau region after a large bathymetric feature that lies within the area.

The triangular Umnak Plateau region lies at the junction of the Bering shelf and the Aleutian Ridge. Water depths throughout 98% of the region are greater than 200 meters and reach a maximum depth of 3200 meters at the base of the continental rise. Numerous submarine canyons are present, which cut deeply into the thick sedimentary section that blankets most of the region. Two of the canyons, Bering and Umnak Canyons, define the landward boundaries for Umnak Plateau. The plateau is a flat-top feature, that lies in 2000 meters of water and is underlain by 3 to 5 km of flat-lying sediment.

The structural framework and geologic history of the Umnak Plateau region are dominated by the two major rock belts that border the region, a eugeosynclinal assemblage of Mesozoic age rocks underlying the Bering shelf and an island-arc suite of Cenozoic rocks that form the Aleutian Ridge. The deep igneous crustal rocks that underlie the Umnak Plateau region may be typical of either the rocks that form these two bordering belts or the oceanic crustal rocks that floor the adjacent abyssal Aleutian Basin.

During Mesozoic time, the Umnak Plateau region was an oceanic area, similar to that found presently in the North Pacific, that bordered an active continental margin. The major constructional phase of the Aleutian Ridge occurred in early Tertiary time and isolated a segment of oceanic crust within the Umnak Plateau region. Since early Tertiray time, four events should be noted:

- Early to middle Tertiary uplift of the oceanic crust beneath the outer part of Umnak Plateau.

- Continuous subsidence of the continental slope within a narrow zone along the landward side of Umnak Plateau.

- Continuous deposition of a 2 to 9 km thick sedimentary section in the deep-water areas and in the summit basins of the Aleutian Ridge.

- Middle to late Cenozoic excavation of the large submarine canyons.

Regional geologic and geophysical mapping indicates that the four requisites for hydrocarbon accumulations may be present in the Umnak Plateau region; source beds, reservoir beds, traps, and an adequate thermal and sedimentation history. However, the presence of hydrocarbons other than methane gas has not been proven by either of the two 900 meter deep holes drilled by Deep Sea Drilling Project (DSDP) on Umnak Plateau. Diatomaceous oozes and mudstones of late Cenozoic age characteristics were found throughout the entire section in these holes.

The hydrocarbon resource assessment for the Umnak Plateau region is that negligible amounts of undiscovered-recoverable oil and gas are present. This assessment is based primarily on current cost relations and technological capabilities for production in deep-water areas. The absence of coarse-grained sediment, typical of reservoirs, at the two shallow penetration drill holes is an additional factor considered in the assessment. Large deposits of oil and gas may be present in the deep-water and Aleutian Ridge summit areas of the Umnak Plateau region; however, these deposits, if present, cannot be recovered at present. Figure 1 shows those areas that have the greatest potential for economic development in the future as production technology advances into the deep water areas.

2

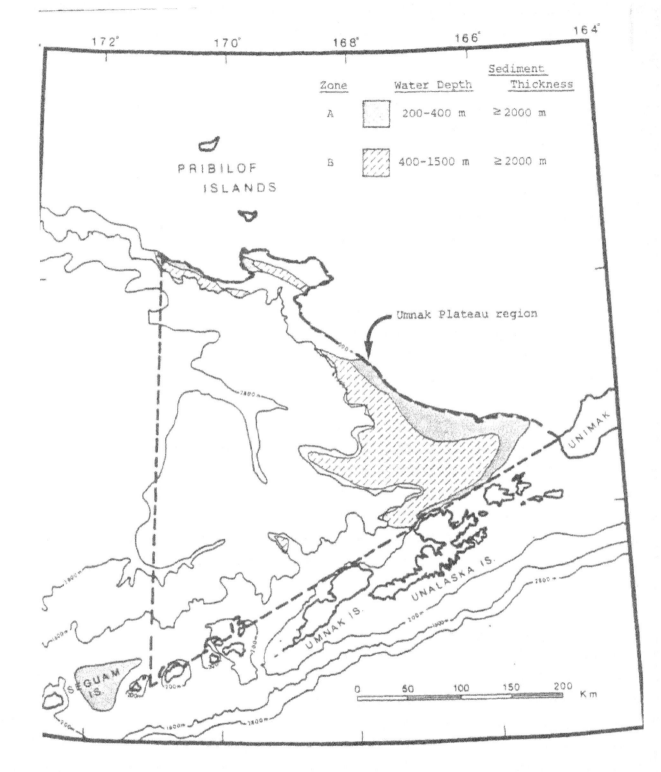

Figure 1. Propective hydrocarbon areas of the Umnak Plateau region. The map shows areas that have the best prospects for hydrocarbon generation (sediment thickness greater than 2000 m or 6560 ft) and are within the present technological limits of deep water exploratory drilling (water depths less than 1500 m or 4920 ft). Zone A shows areas where offshore production is currently possible (water depths less than 400 m or 1300 ft). Zone B covers those areas where exploratory drilling is also presently possible.

Based on present information, the Umnak Plateau region must be considered a potentially important future hydrocarbon province. Further geologic and geophysical investigations are required to specify the location, amount, and types of hydrocarbons, if any, that may be present.

INTRODUCTION

Location

This report summarizes geological and geophysical data from the deep-
water (greater than 200m) region of the St. George Basin lease sale area
#70. The shallow-water region is discussed in detail by Marlow and others
(1979a) in a companion report. The triangular deep-water region lies at the
junction of the Bering shelf and the Aleutian Ridge (Fig. 2). This region is
bounded on the northeast by the 200 m bathymetric contour that defines the
edge of the Bering shelf, on the southeast by a meandering line that lies 3
miles north of the Aleutian Islands, and on the west by the 171°W longitude
meridian. Hereafter, this triangular region is referred to as the Umnak
Plateau region. The name is derived from a major bathymetric feature, Umnak
Plateau, that covers most of the region.

Publically available data

Numerous types of geological and geophysical data have been collected in
the St. George Basin lease sale area. The following information, in addition
to those data listed by Marlow and others (1979a) for the Bering shelf area,
is available for the Umnak Plateau region:

Subsurface geology (Creager and Scholl and others, 1973; Marlow and others
1979b)

Geologic map (Beikman, 1978)

Gravity map (Watts, 1975)

Sonobuoy reflection/refraction data (Childs and Cooper, 1979)

Seismic reflection records (single-channel): (Scholl and Hopkins, 1967;
Scholl and others, 1969, 1976; Marlow and others, 1976; Gardner and
Vallier, 1977a, 1977b, 1978)

With exception of the summit areas of the Aleutian Ridge, the Umnak

5

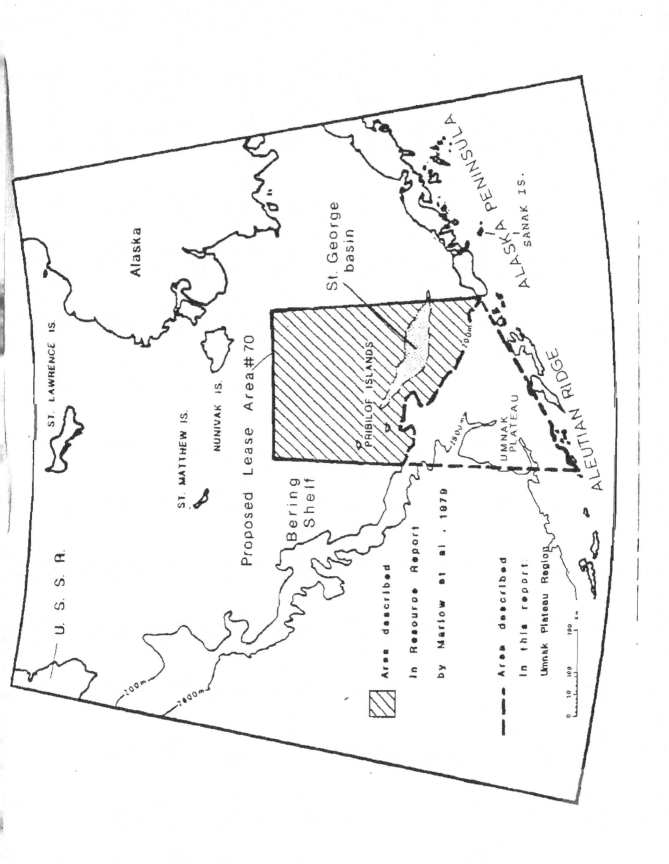

Plateau region is covered by more than 200 meters of water. In nearly 80% of the region, the water depths exceed 1500 meters, the maximum water depth for commercial hydrocarbon drilling exploration (O&GJ, 1979). Most of the region must be considered a future hydrocarbon province because of these extreme water depths, even if the existence of significant hydrocarbons is confirmed. Detailed environmental investigations have not been funded in these extreme water depths, consequently this report presents only the regional tectonic framework of the Umnak Plateau region. The anticipated environmental hazards in the region are briefly discussed, and the reader is referred to Marlow and others (1979a) for a compilation of the environmental studies that have been conducted along the outer edge of the Bering shelf.

Regional Tectonic Setting

The Bering shelf lies along the northeastern edge of the Umnak Plateau region and is a broad continental platform that is underlain by deformed Mesozoic and Cenozoic rocks similar to those found on the adjacent Alaska Peninsula (Marlow and others, 1979a). The outer edge of the southern shelf is incised by deep rift-basins, such as St. George Basin, that have been filled with upper Mesozoic and Cenozoic sediment. A basement ridge of presumed shallow-water Jurassic rocks, Pribilof Ridge, forms the structural underpinnings of the outer shelf edge. This offshore ridge connects with the Black Hills ridge on the Alaska Peninsula (Marlow and others, 1979a, Fig. 4). The Black Hills-Pribilof ridge is one of several Mesozoic features that change direction from a northeast-southwest trend along the Alaska Peninsula to a northwest-southeast trend along the southern Bering shelf.

Mesozoic structures form the northeast boundary of the Umnak Plateau region, however, the southeast boundary is delineated by Cenozoic structures associated with the Aleutian Ridge (Marlow and others, 1973; Scholl and others, 1975a). Tertiary igneous and sedimentary rocks are found along the entire length of the Aleutian Ridge-Alaska Peninsula (Beikman, 1978). The westernmost exposure of pre-Cenozoic rocks on the Alaska peninsula is at Sanak Island, near the junction of the Aleutian Ridge and the Alaska Peninsula. The exclusive occurrence of Cenozoic rocks on the Aleutian Ridge has been used as evidence that the ridge formed in early Tertiary time and did not exist during Mesozoic time (Scholl and others, 1975a).

The Aleutian Ridge presently separates oceanic crustal rocks of the Pacific Ocean basin from oceanic crustal rocks of the Aleutian Basin, Bering Sea. During late Mesozoic time, the oceanic crust of the Aleutian Basin, was part of a much larger oceanic plate that abutted against the Bering Sea continental margin. The development of the Aleutian Ridge in early Tertiary time trapped a piece of this oceanic plate in the Aleutian Basin. The oceanic crust of the Aleutian Basin has received a thick accumulation of Tertiary sediment and this sediment-thickened crust now forms the western boundary of the Umnak Plateau region.

The structural fabric of the Umnak Plateau region is dominated by the alignment of the two major foldbelts that border the region, a Mesozoic eugeosynclinal foldbelt underlying the Bering shelf and a Cenozoic island arc that forms the Aleutian Ridge. The nature of the basement rocks that lie beneath the Umnak Plateau region may, however, be similar to the igneous oceanic crustal rocks that lie beneath the adjacent abyssal Aleutian Basin.

8

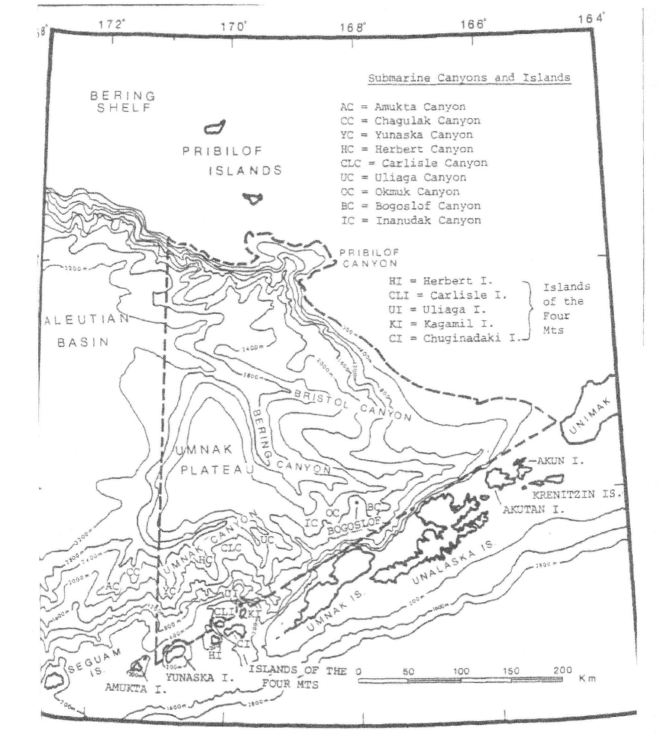

Figure 3. Index map showing physiographic features of the Umnak Plateau region.

GEOLOGIC FRAMEWORK

Geomorphic Setting

Umnak Plateau and Continental Slope

The Umnak Plateau region (Fig. 3) is incised by numerous submarine
canyons that head on the summit of the Aleutian Ridge and on the outer edge of
the Bering Shelf. The two large canyons, Pribilof Canyon and Bering Canyon,
have been described in detail by Scholl and others (1970), and a physiographic
diagram of these two canyons is shown in Figure 4. The physiographic diagrams
show that the north side of the Aleutian Ridge is deeply incised and has
numerous steep walled and narrow canyons (Fig. 4a). In contrast the
southeastern part of the Bering slope has gentle relief and is cut by two long
meandering canyons, Bering Canyon and Bristol Canyon.

Bering Canyon is nearly 400 km long and traverses the Umnak Plateau
region in a westerly direction from its head near Unimak Island to the inner
side of Umnak Plateau. At this point the canyon turns north, joins with
Bristol Canyon, and debouches onto the floor of the Aleutian Basin near the
mouth of Pribilof Canyon. The volume of Bering Canyon, as determined from the
material missing from the continental margin is 4300 km^3, an enormous figure
in comparison to the 1300 km^3 volume Pribilof Canyon and the normal 500 km^3
volume of most other large submarine canyons (Scholl and others, 1970).
Pribilof Canyon, exhibits a characteristic bathymetric T-shape. This shape
results from the headward bifurcation of the canyon axis.

Aleutian Ridge

The southern boundary of the Umnak Plateau region falls along the crestal
area of the southwest-trending Aleutian Ridge (Fig. 2). Within the region,
the base of the ridge occurs at depths ranging from 3000 to about 200m; the
position of the base, is coincident with the axes of Bering Canyon (off Figur

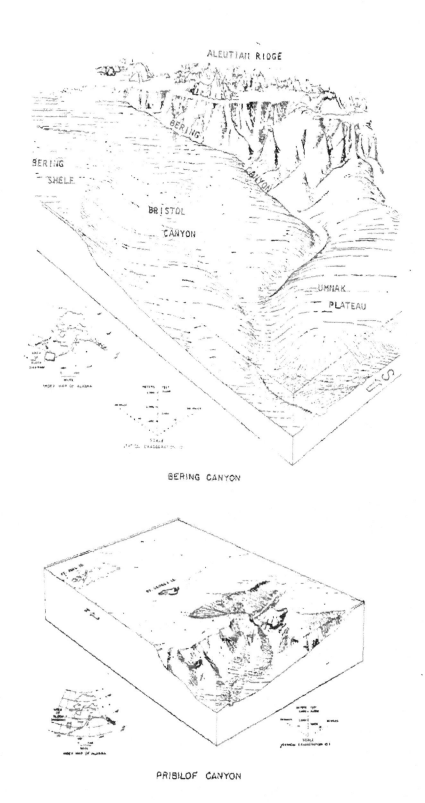

Figure 4. Physiographic diagrams of Bering and Pribilof Canyons.

Unalaska and Umnak Islands) and Umnak Canyon (off the Islands of Four

Mountains and Yunaska Island; Figs. 3, 5). Segments of the ridge flank slope

toward these canyons at angles exceeding 10°, although the typical slope is

between 3° and 6°. The average slope angle is only about 2° where Umnak

Plateau borders the ridge north of Umnak Island. The flank of the ridge in

this area merges with the plateau's summit platform at a depth of 2000 m, but

the geomorphic boundary is not sharply defined (Fig. 5).

Numerous submarine canyons dissect the northern flank of the Aleutian

Ridge (Fig. 3). These canyons are tributary to either Bering or Umnak Canyons

and have been incised into the ridge's flank by sediment-ladened currents

originating near the ridge's summit area (Scholl and others 1975b).

The summit or crestal area of the Aleutian Ridge, is actually a wide

plateau or platform that rises above a water depth of 200 m (Fig. 5). The

Aleutian Islands, which include lofty and active stratocone volcanoes, rise

above the summit platform. Some of the smaller Aleutian Islands (for example

the Baby Islands of Akutan Pass) near the southern boundary of the Umnak

Plateau region are raised areas of the summit platform. All of the large

islands in this region; Unmak, Akun, Akutan, Unalaska, Umnak, the Islands of

the Four Mountains, Yunaska, Chagulak, and Amukta Islands (Fig. 3), comprise,

or are totally formed by, active or dormant volcanoes (Coats, 1950). One

small island, Bogoslof Island is an active volcano that rises from he ridge's

northern flank (Byers, 1959).

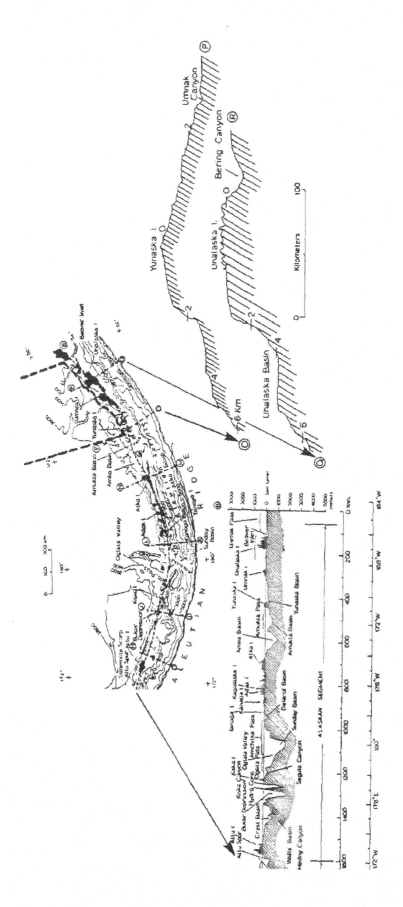

Figure 5. Physiographic profiles across and along the crest of the
Aleutian ridge.

Geology of Umnak Plateau Region

Umnak Plateau and Continental Slope

Geologic data for the Umnak Plateau region is sparse (Figs. 6, 7) and is limited to outcrops on the Pribilof Islands and Aleutain Islands (Beikman, 1978), two Deep-Sea Drilling Project (DSDP) sites on Umnak Plateau (Creager, Scholl and others, 1973), rocks dredged from the Bering slope (Hopkins and Scholl, 1969; Marlow and others, 1979b; Vallier and others, 1979), and shallow-penetration cores along the eastern part of Umnak Plateau (see Marlow and others, 1979a).

Only the upper 973 meters of the 2 to 8 km thick sedimentary sequence that blankets most of the Umnak Plateau region have been drilled by DSDP on Umnak Plateau. The oldest rocks recovered are early Pliocene or late Miocene in age (Fig. 8). The sediment in the upper 600 meters of the DSDP sites is primarily diatomaceous ooze with silt, clay, ash and limestone. Below 600 to 650 meters, the diatomaceous sediment is diagenetically altered to lithified clayey siltstone. The diatoms are not preserved in the altered siltstone consequently age determinations cannot be made for these rocks.

Diatomaceous clay and siltstone of late Pliocene to late Miocene age has been dredged from outcrops along the inner wall of Pribilof Canyon. Vallier and others (in press) indicate that most of the Miocene and younger rocks found in Pribilof Canyon and beneath Umnak Plateau have been derived from sediment sources on the Aleutian Ridge, rather than on the Alaska Peninsula Transport of this sediment has occurred mostly by longshore drift, debris flows, and turbidity currents. Vallier and others (in press) also believe that the paleo-depositional environment for the rocks in Pribilof Canyon and beneath Umank Plateau was similar to the present depositional environment.

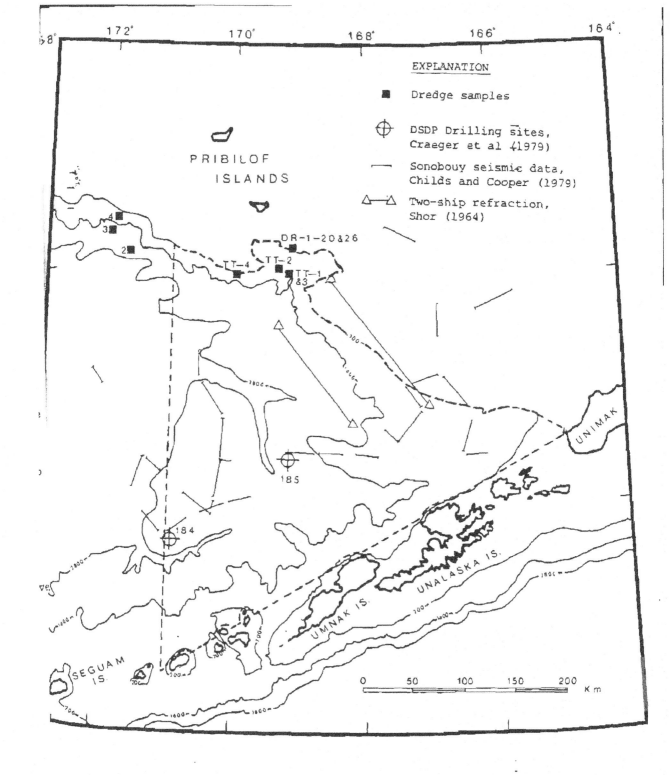

Figure 6. Geologic and seismic refraction sampling sites.

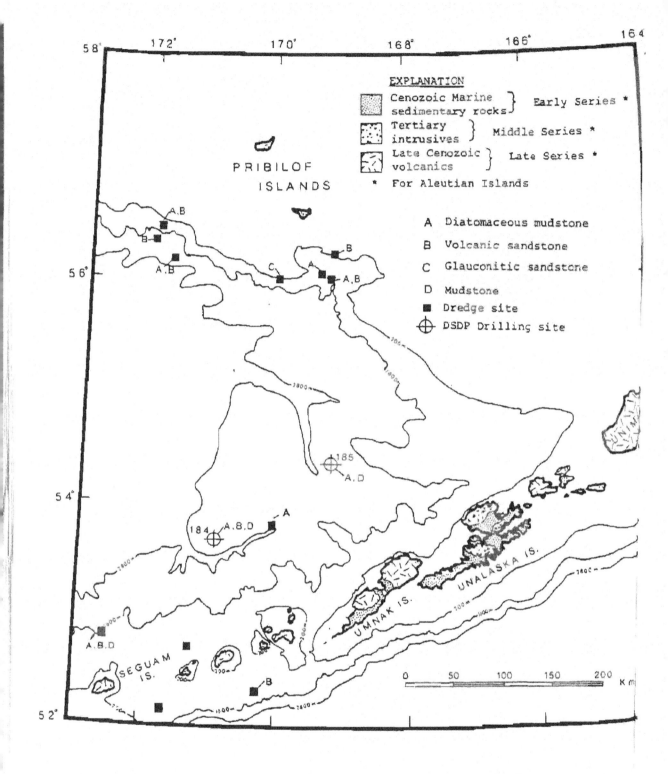

Figure 7. Geologic data for the Umnak Plateau region.

SITE 184

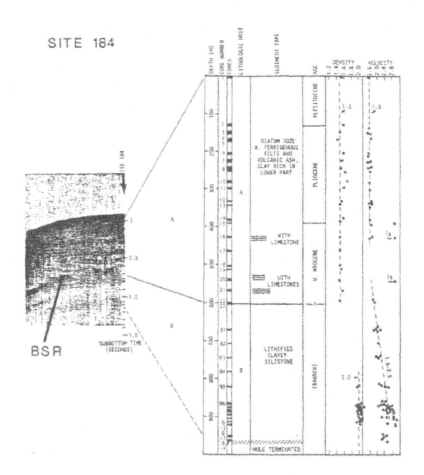

BSR

SITE 185

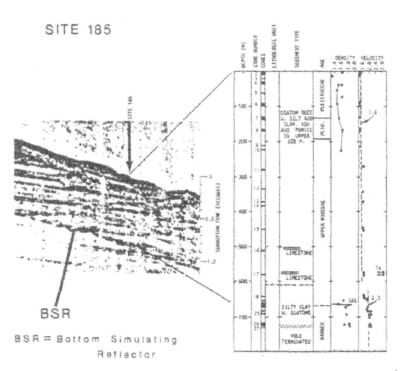

BSR

BSR = Bottom Simulating
Reflector

Figure 8. DSDP drilling sections at sites 184 and 185.

Basement rocks beneath Umnak Plateau have not been sampled and the origin

of these rocks, whether oceanic, continental, or island-arc rocks, is unknown.

North of Umnak Plateau acoustic basement has been sampled at the base of the

continental slope (sites TT-2, TT-3,TT-4, Fig. 6). These rocks consist of

sandstone of late Jurassic (?) age (Marlow and others, 1979b). South of Umnak

Plateau, the acoustic basement can be traced from outcrops of Tertiary

volcanic rocks on the Aleutian Ridge to the base of the Plateau (Scholl and

others, 1975a). West of the plateau, the acoustic basement in the Aleutian

Basin is believed, on the basis of seismic refraction and magnetic studies

(Cooper and others, 1976), to be oceanic basalt of Cretaceous age. The

acoustic basement can be traced from the Aleutian Basin to beneath Umnak

Plateau. Based on these three observations, any one of three rock types of

different age and lithology (late Jurassic sandstone, Tertiary volcanic rocks,

or Cretaceous oceanic basalt) are likely candidates for the basement rocks

that underlie Umnak Plateau.

Aleutian Ridge

Attempts to decipher the geologic history of the Aleutian Ridge are

complicated by many factors, not the least of which is that only 0.1 percent

of the ridge's surface area is subaerially exposed. Late Cenozoic volcanoes

constitute about 30 percent of the exposed insular area, and at least half of

the remainder is buried beneath a concealing mantle of tundra, volcanic ash,

or glacial drift. Offshore geophysical information is limited to widely

spaced lines of magnetic and gravimetric data and single-channel seismic-

reflection profiles (Fig. 9). Information gleaned from rocks dredged at

approximately 50 sites along the length of the ridge, and cores from

subsurface sections drilled at DSDP sites 186, 187, and 189, all near but

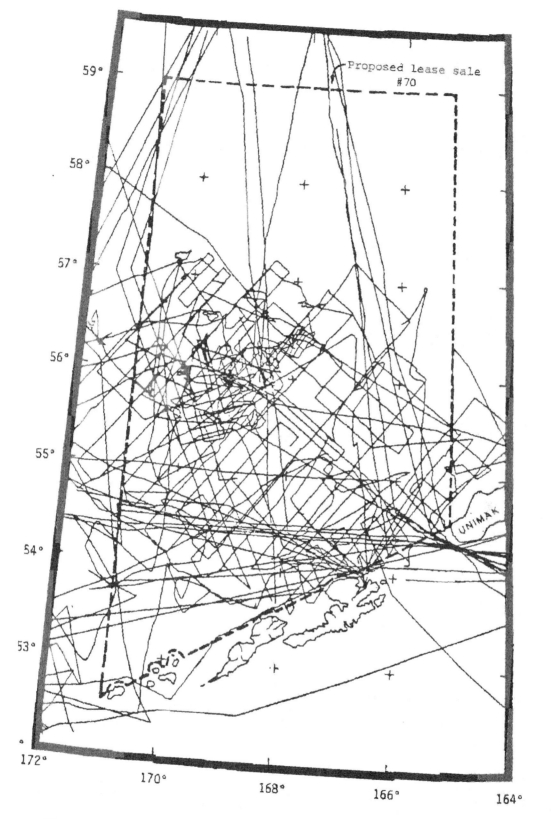

Figure 9. Geophysical trackline data within lease sale area #70.

seaward of the ridge's insular slopes, constitute the meager store of available offshore geologic information.

Marlow and others (1973), and Scholl and others (1975a, b) summarize much of this limited knowledge and attempt to synthesize a coherent picture. Four informally named rock units have been recognized that appear to have regional application only along the crestal region and upper flanks of the ridge: the igneous and sedimentary rocks of the initial, early, middle, and late series (Scholl and others, 1975a).

The initial series is inferred to be mafic volcanic and intrusive masses of latest Cretaceous or earliest Tertiary age that form the bulk of the Aleutian Ridge. Shor (1964) assigns a velocity of 5.5 km/sec to these rocks on the basis of refraction work (see also Ludwig and others, 1971). Outcrops that are unequivocally those of the initial series are not known.

The oldest rocks exposed on the ridge may be the basaltic flows of the basement rocks defined by Gates and others (1971) on Attu Island, or the Finger Bay Volcanics (Coats, 1956a) that form much of Adak Island (Fig. 7). The volcanic rocks on Attu and Adak Islands are associated with thick sections of tuffaceous and terrigenous sedimentary rocks; these volcanic and sedimentary sequences form the early series, a designation originally used by Wilcox (1959). Rocks of the early series are widespread and crop out on most of the large islands of the Aleutian Islands, including those bordering the southern boundary of the Umnak Plateau region. Characteristically, beds of the early series, although only broadly deformed, are extensively altered by low-grade thermal metamorphism (Gates and other, 1954; Coats, 1956b; Wilcox, 1959). The early series is the oldest unit that has been dated. Its interbedded volcanic and sedimentary rocks accumulated from middle Eocene (Scholl and others, 1970) through early Miocene time (Drewes and others, 1961) in crestal basins and along the upper flanks of the ridge. Although they are chiefly of marine origin, rocks of the early series formed after sectors of the ridge had built above sea level and, presumably, after its initial rapid growth by mafic volcanism had greatly slowed 50-55 m.y. ago.

The early series near the Umnak Plateau region is represented by the Unalaska Formation of Unalaska Island, and equivalent rocks on nearby Umnak Island (Drewes and others, 1961; Byers, 1959). Sparse information implies that these broadly deformed, thermally altered and intruded rocks are of early Miocene age. They presumably form the basement rocks underlying the northern flank of the Aleutian Ridge.

Rocks of the middle series unconformably overlie or intrude units of the early series. Middle series rocks of volcanic origin may not be widely distributed on the Aleutian Islands; they are best known from Amchitka Island where they crop out as the mostly volcanic Chitka Point Formation (Powers and others, 1960; Carr and others, 1970, 1971). Exposed volcanic members of the middle series are typically shallow-marine or subaerial accumulations of andesitic composition that have not been significantly altered or greatly deformed. Plutonic bodies, mostly of granodioritic composition, are related temporally to these extrusives. Both rock types have K-Ar ages of middle Miocene age (i.e., 10.5 to 16 m.y.; Marlow and others, 1973). The middle series along the crestal region of the ridge is a group of rocks which formed during the waning phases of a moderate tectonic event that slightly deformed and uplifted the underlying marine rocks of the early series.

Little is known about offshore beds of the middle series (middle Miocene age), because they have been sampled with certainty only at dredge stations (USGS cruise S6-79-NP) north and south of Amlia Island, west of the Umnak Plateau region. On the basis of sections drilled at DSDP Sites 184, 185, 186,

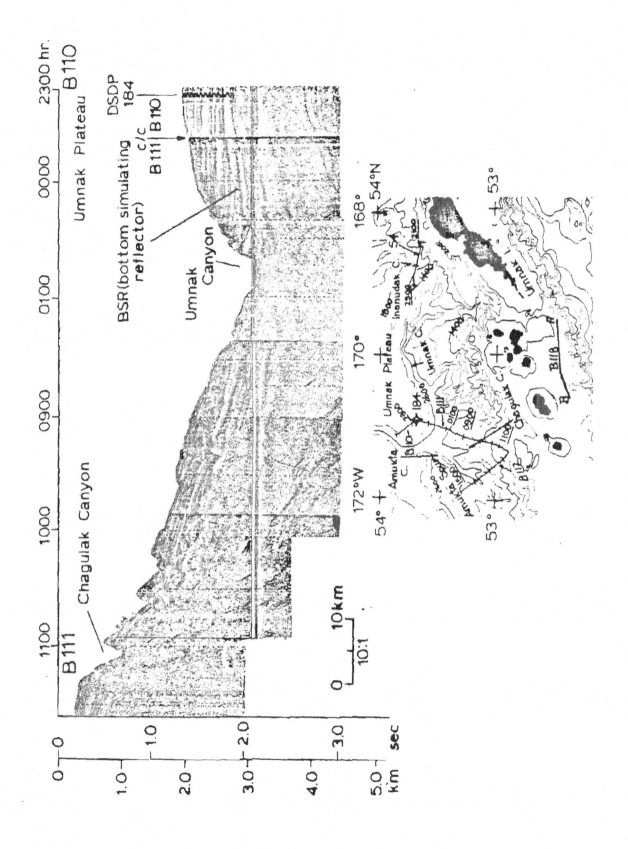

and 189 (Fig. 7), and regional correlation of stratigraphic sequences resolved on reflection profiles, slightly deformed middle series beds are inferred to overlie early series rocks that form the basement of the ridge flanks (Figs. 10, 11).

Igneous and sedimentary rocks of late Miocene through Holocene age constitute the late series. These rocks are unaltered and in most areas only gently deformed (Fig. 7). Insular exposures of the late series are limited to the effusive andesitic outpourings of the Aleutian volcanoes. Although some of these volcanic centers first erupted in the latest Miocene, K-Ar dates of flows and associated rocks and the paleontologically determined ages of ash falls recorded at Bering Sea and North Pacific DSDP sites, document that most of the volcanism was post-Miocene in age (Marlow and others, 1973; Scholl and Creager, 1973). Large volumes of sediment of the late series beds have accumulated in summit or crestal basins (Fig. 12). These basins are grabens or fault-bordered depressions (Marlow and others, 1970, 1973). Beneath the southwestern corner of the Umnak Plateau region late series beds as much as 1500 m thick may mantle the ridge's northern flank. Although a large fraction of this depositional debris is volcanic ash and diatom ooze, much of its bulk is terrigenous detritus derived from the crestal region of the ridge.

The late series accumulated during a time when extensional rifting formed many of the ridge's summit basins (Fig. 12) and explosive volcanism created the arcuate chain of the Aleutian stratovolcanoes (Fig. 13). Beneath the ridge's summit platform, sediment of the late series rest unconformably above older rocks of the early series and possibly also the middle series. However, beneath the flanks of the ridge, within the Umnak Plateau region, late series beds are thought to rest conformably above middle series units (Fig. 10, 11) A similar conformable relation may exist within the thick sedimentary sequences

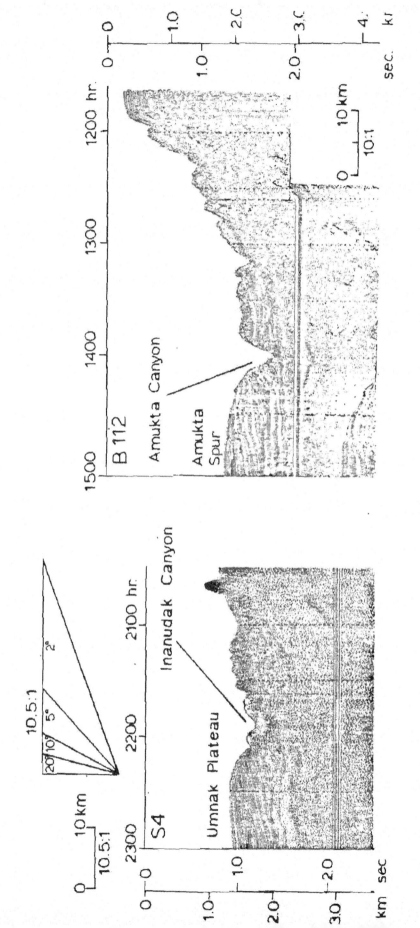

Figure 11. Reflection profiles S4 and B112 on the north flank of Aleutian ... See figure 10 for location.

filling some of the summit basins, one of which, Amukta Basin, is partly included in the Umank Plateau region (Fig. 12).

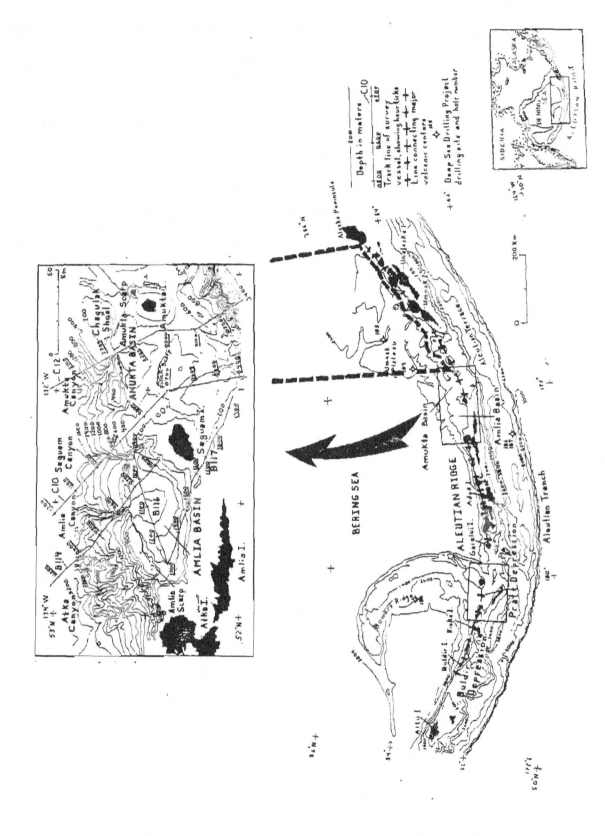

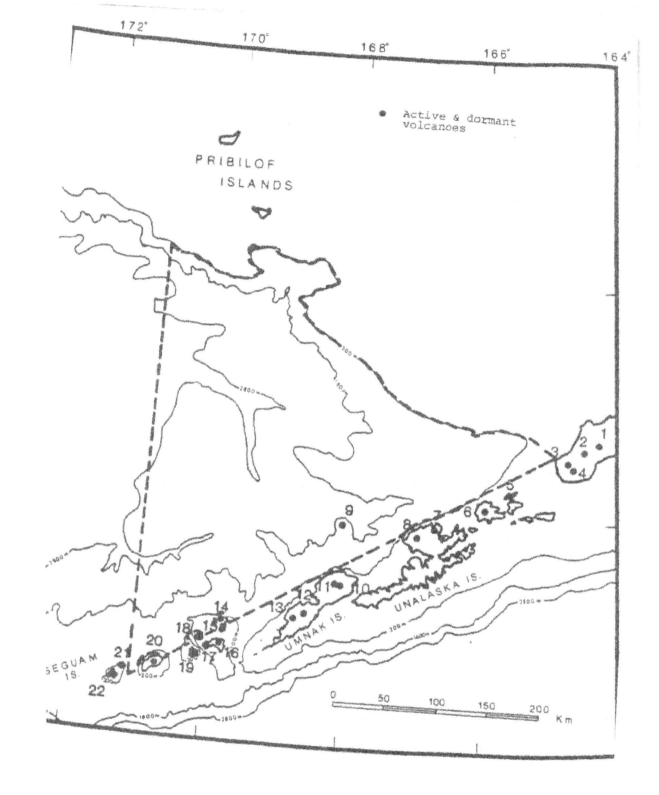

Figure 13. Index map of active and dormant volcanoes of the Aleutian Ridge near the Umnak Plateau region. Volcano names are given in Table 1.

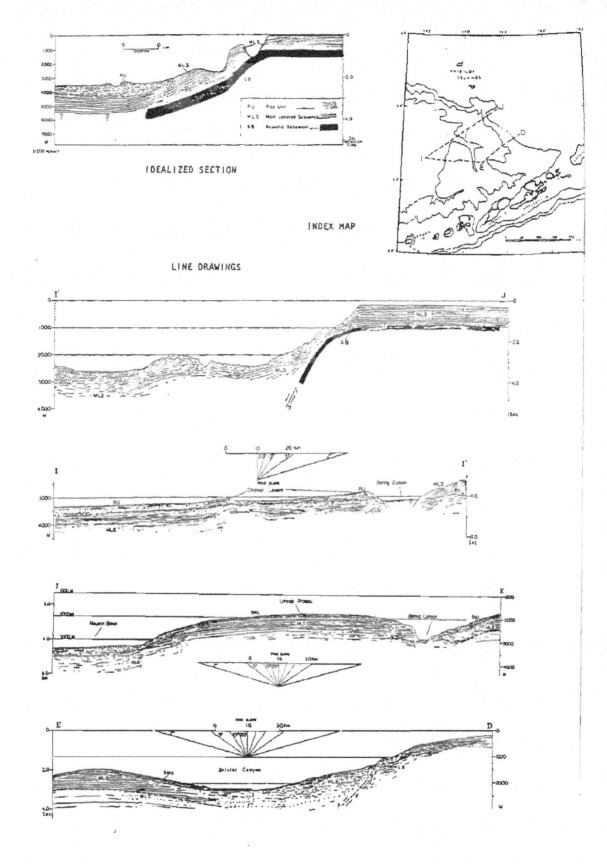

Figure 14. Seismic reflection profiles across the Umnak Plateau region (from Scholl and others, 1968).

STRUCTURAL FRAMEWORK

Seismic Reflection/Refraction Data

Several thousand kilometers of single-channel seismic-reflection records have been collected over the Umnak Plateau region (Figs. 9) and many of these records have been described by Scholl and others (1968, 1970); Scholl and Hopkins (1969); Marlow and others (1976, 1977). Seismic refraction data are limited to the 2-ship refraction profiles of Shor (1964) along the outer Bering shelf and to the sonobuoy studies of Childs and Cooper (1979a, b) over Umnak Plateau (Fig. 6).

Scholl and others (1968), on the basis of pre-1968 seismic reflection records, have defined four acoustic units for the Umnak Plateau region: Acoustic Basement (AB), Main Layered Sequence (MLS), Rise Unit (RU), and Surface Mantling Unit (SMU; Fig. 14). More recent seismic reflection records generally show the same acoustic units but have greater resolution of sub-units within the MLS.

Acoustic basement comprises Mesozoic sedimentary rocks beneath the Bering shelf (Vp=4.9 to 5.3 km/sec) but is of unknown age and composition under Umnak Plateau (V=3.4 to 4.8 km/sec). The main layered sequence forms the bulk of the sedimentary section and is often several kilometers thick. This sequence consists of several distinct sub-units of flat-lying sediment of Cenozoic age (V_p=1.6 to 3.4 km/sec). The rise unit is primarily Pleistocene turbidites that cover the MLS in the abyssal Aleutian Basin and that pinch out at the base of the continental slope. The flanks of the submarine canyons that cut through Umnak Plateau are covered by the surface mantling unit. The diatomaceous and terrigenous sediment of the SMU have been deposited during periods of canyon cutting and are separated from the underlying MLS by an angular unconformity.

Table 1: Volcanoes Adjacent to Umnak Plateau region, Umnak to Amukta Islands, Alaska

	Volcano	Island	Elevation (m)	Activity
1.	Shishaldin	Unimak	2,860	active
2.	Fisher	Unimak	1,095	active
3.	Westdahl Peak	Unimak	1,560	dormant
4.	Pogromni	Unimak	2,002	active
5.	Mt. Gilbert	Akun	810	dormant
6.	Akutan	Akutan	1,300	active
7.	Tabletop Mtn.	Unalaska	800	dormant
8.	Mt. Makushin	Unalaska	2,036	active
9.	Bogoslof	Bogoslof	100	active
10.	Tulik	Umnak	1,253	dormant
11.	Okmok	Umnak	1,073	active
12.	Mt. Recheschnoi	Umnak	1,985	dormant
13.	Mt. Vseuldof	Umnak	210	active
14.	Kagamil	Kagamil	893	active
15.	Uliaga	Uliaga	888	dormant
16.	Tana	Chuginadak	1,170	dormant
17.	Mt. Cleveland	Chuginadak	1,730	active
18.	Carlisle	Carlisle	1,896	active
19.	Herbert	Herbert	1,291	dormant
20.	Yunaska	Yunaska	680	active ?
21.	Chagulak	Chagulak	1,143	dormant
22.	Amukta	Amukta	1,656	active
23	Sequam	Sequam	1,050	active

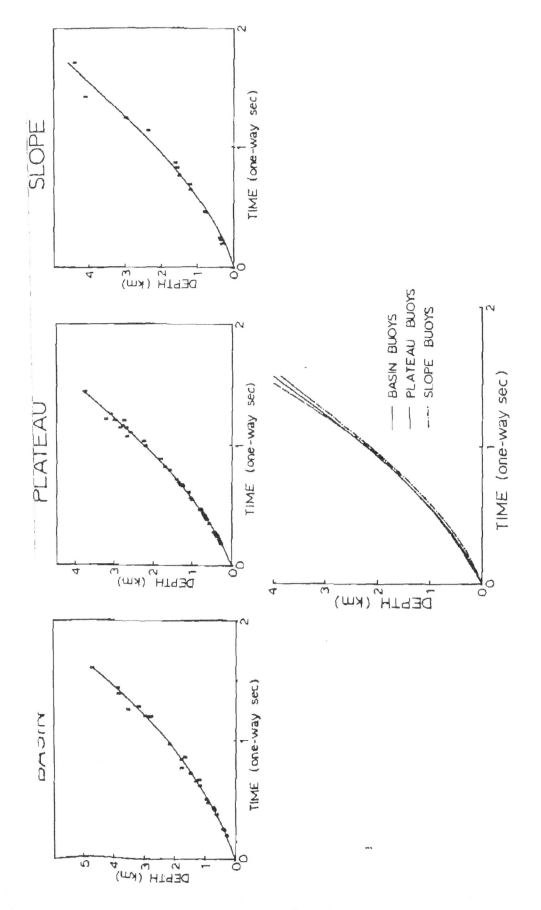

Figure 15. Comparison of depth versus reflection time for three physiographic areas in the Umnak Plateau region.

Sedimentary and Igneous Crustal Sections

Sonobuoy studies over Umnak Plateau (Childs and others, 1979) have resolved three velocity layers within the MLS. The shallowest layer is Holocene to late Miocene age and has interval velocities between 1.6 and 2.0 km/sec. The second layer is middle to late Miocene age and has velocities between 2.1 and 2.8 km/sec. The two layers are separated by a diagenetic boundary (Hein and others, 1978) that is also a highly-reflective horizon termed the Bottom Simulating Reflector (BSR; Fig. 8). The BSR occurs at a sub-bottom depth of 0.7 to 0.8 km and mimics the seafloor topography. This reflector is also an areally extensive refracting horizon (V_p=2.3 to 2.6 km/sec) beneath the plateau and lower slope area. The third velocity layer (V_p=2.5 to 3.4 km/sec) lies below the Miocene section and contains rocks of unknown age. A small but areally extensive velocity inversion (less than 0.2 km/sec) occurs between layers two and three. The inversion, which is observed on nine sonobuoy records over Umnak Plateau, may represent a lithologic change from altered diatomaceous to terrigeneous sediment. A synthesesis of all sonobuoy reflection time-depth data (fig. 15) shows that each of the physiographic provinces of the Umnak Plateau region (Aleutian Basin, Umnak Plateau, continental slope) have similar time-depth, or velocity, sections.

The interpretive drawings of seismic reflection records across the Umnak Plateau region (Fig. 14) illustrate the generally good continuity of the reflective horizons within the main layered sequence (MLS). Prior to the erosion and excavation of the large submarine canyons, the MLS was probably continuous across the entire region. Presently, the sedimentary section beneath Umnak Plateau is almost totally isolated from the surrounding areas

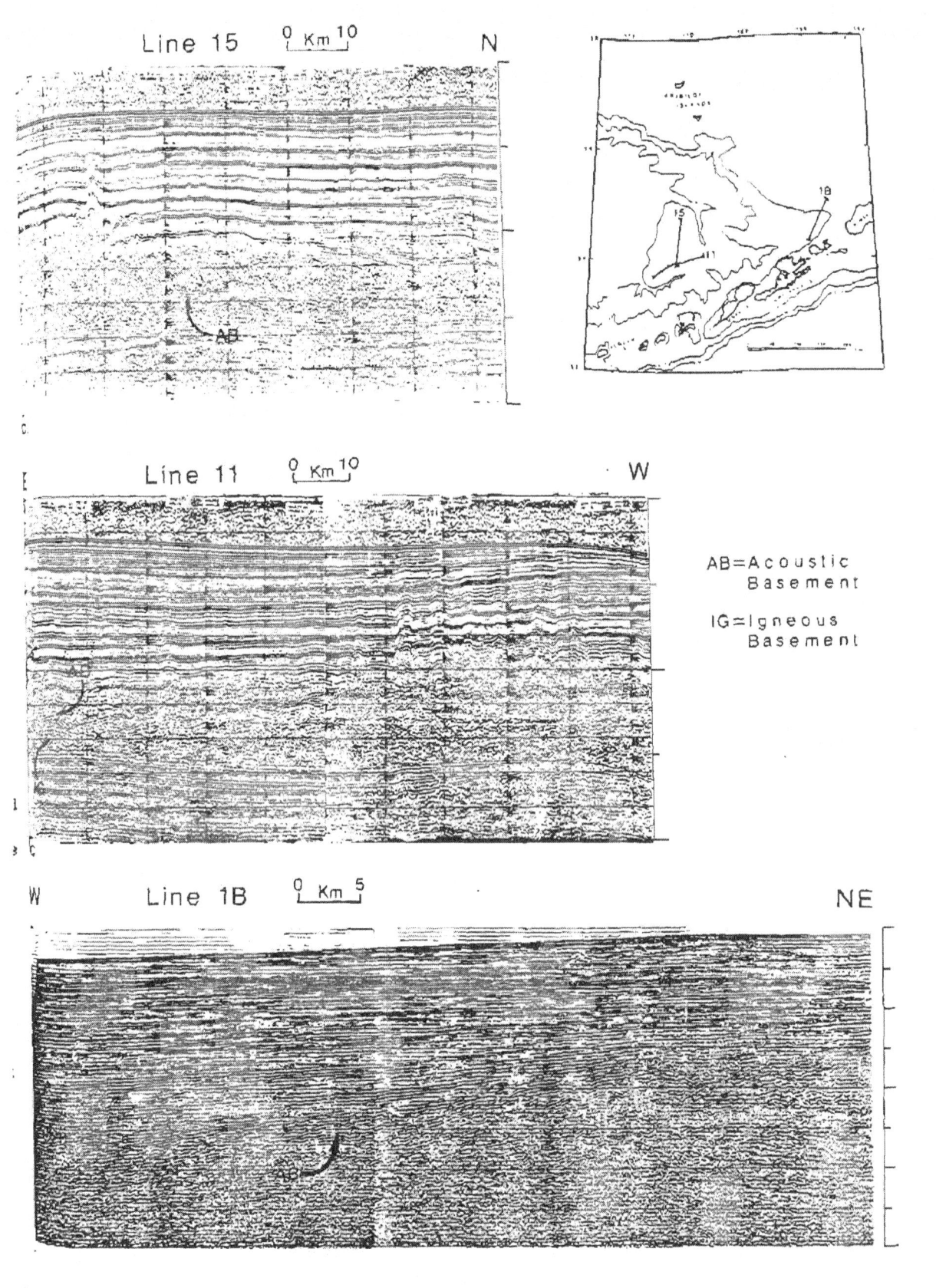

Figure 16. Seismic reflection records across the Umnak Plateau region. Profiles 11 and 15 are single channel records; line 1B is a multi-channel record.

the intervening Bering and Umnak canyons (profile I-E, Fig. 14). The MLS
generally is not severely deformed except in areas of steep slopes, such as
within the submarine canyons and along the upper continental slope.
Reflectors in these areas are sometimes discontinuous, arched, and folded by
slumping and faulting.

Deep acoustic horizons within the MLS can be seen on large-volume airgun
seismic reflection records (Fig. 16). These records show that the acoustic
basement is often buried by as much as 8 km of sediment and is not always a
distinct reflecting horizon (line 1B, Fig. 16). The records across Umnak
Plateau show that the acoustic basement surface has irregular relief (line 11)
and that unconformities may be present in the sedimentary section (line 15).
The depth to the top of acoustic basement, as determined from the seismic data
(Cooper and others, in press), is shown in the structure-contour map on figure
17; a companion isopach map that shows the total thickness of sediment above
acoustic basement is illustrated in figure 18.

The structure-contour and isopach maps indicate that the thickest parts
of the sedimentary section (4 to 8 km thick) are found in deep basement
depressions that lie beneath the upper continental slope along the north side
of the Aleutian Ridge and along the southern part of the Bering shelf.
Beneath other parts of the Umnak Plateau region the acoustic basement surface
forms ridges, troughs, and isolated piercement features with a relief of 1.5
to 2.5 km. The sediment thickness in these parts generally ranges from 2 to 4
km.

Sonobuoy studies (Childs and others, 1979) indicate that the igneous
basement may lie 1.0 to 1.5 km below the acoustic basement; consequently, the
depths and thicknesses for the sedimentary section may be 1.0 to 1.5 km deeper
and thicker than shown on the structure-contour and isopach maps. The Figure

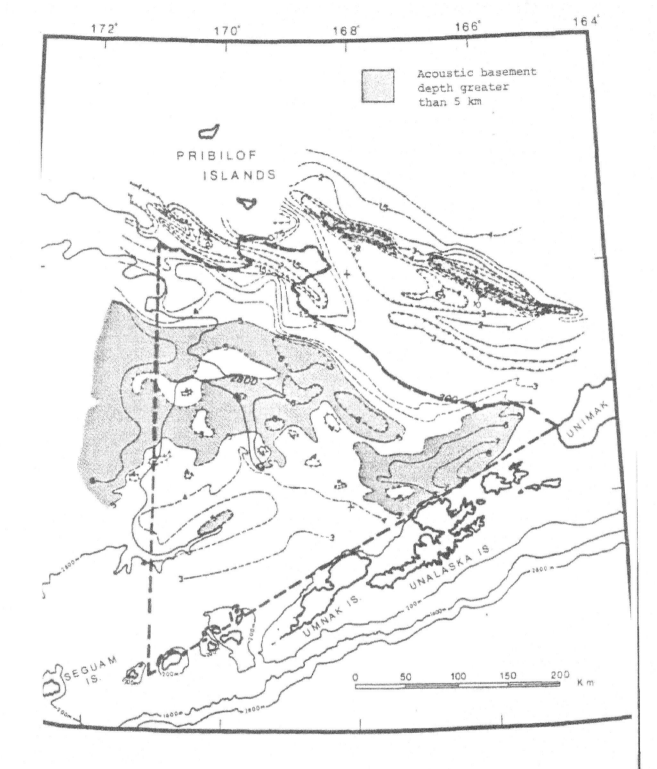

Figure 17. Structure-contour map showing the depth from sea level to acoustic basement.

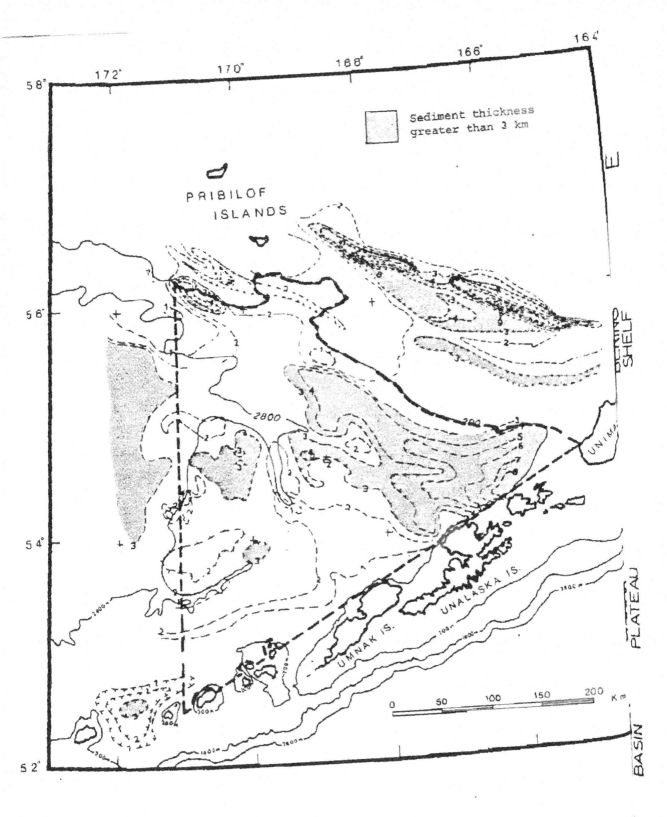

Figure 18. Isopach map showing the thickness of sediment above acoustic basement.

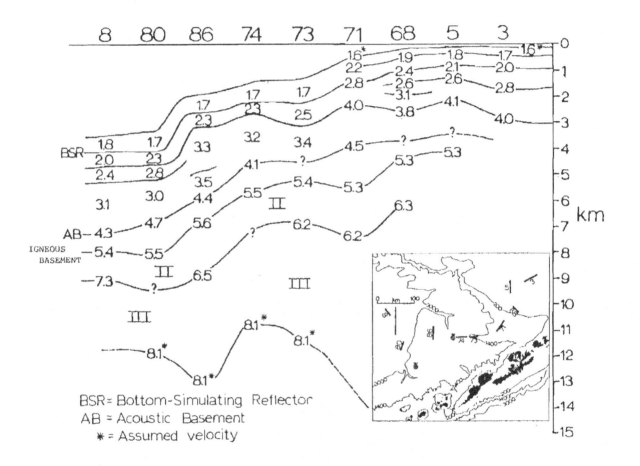

BSR = Bottom-Simulating Reflector
AB = Acoustic Basement
 * = Assumed velocity

acoustic basement has a refraction velocity of 3.4 to 4.8 km/sec, velocities
that are more typical of sedimentary rocks than of igenous rocks. A deeper
interface below acoustic basement that is commonly observed on the sonobuoy
records has a refraction velocity of 5.0 to 5.3 km/sec (basalt ?). This
interface is usually not associated with a continuous reflecting horizon.
Where a sub-acoustic basement reflecting horizon is present (line 11, Fig. 16)
the horizon does not conform with the overlying acoustic basement reflector
and thus indicates local thickening and thinning of a sub-acoustic basement
layer.

The crustal structure beneath Umnak Plateau is more like the oceanic
areas of the Aleutian Basin than the continental margin of the Bering shelf.
The velocity (V_p>5.3 km/sec) and thickness of igneous crustal layers under the
outer part of the plateau are similar to the Aleutian Basin although the depth
to the top of the igneous crust is 2 to 3 km shallower under the plateau (Fig.
19). The major increase in total crustal thickness (sea floor to top of
mantle) occurs on the landward, rather than the seaward, side of the
plateau. On the landward side, the crust thickens from 10 km (buoy 86, Fig.
19) to 21 km (near buoy 71, Fig. 19; Shor, 1964). The velocity structure of
the igneous crust also changes beneath Umnak Plateau. The two layer oceanic
crust (V_p=5.5, 6.8 km/sec) abruptly becomes a two-layer continental (or
transitional) crust (V_p=5.0, 6.2 km/sec) 75 km east of the base of the
plateau. This change is apparent from the bimodal distribution of velocities
beneath the plateau (Fig. 20).

Diapirs

Numerous diapirs have been documented beneath Umnak Plateau (Fig. 21).
Scholl and Marlow (1970) have studied three of these diapirs and conclude tha

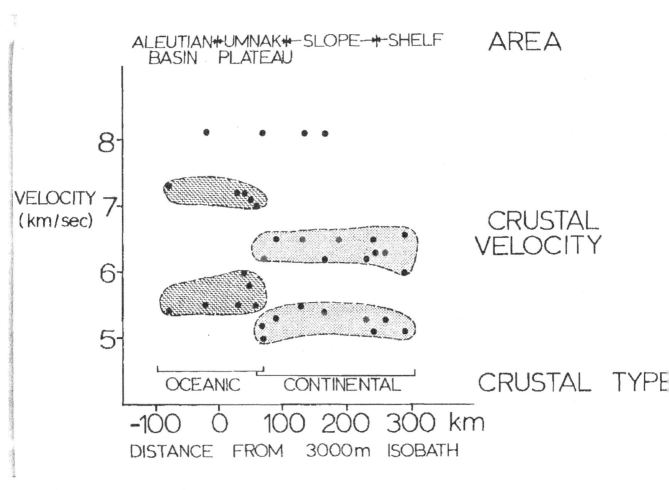

they are cored by either shale or salt. Because shale is prominent in the sedimentary section they favor a core of mobil shale. In more recent seismic reflection records, the diapirs occur as both isolated features and as diapiric ridges or clusters (Fig. 16). Isolated diapirs are the more common features, however, and these features generally have a relief of 500 to 1500 meters. The larger features are more common around the perimeter of the plateau. Childs and others (1979) believe that the source material for these diapirs may be from the variable thickness layer that lies directly beneath acoustic basement and that the variable thickness layer may be a mobile shale unit.

Folding and Faulting

Most of Umnak Plateau is covered by relatively undeformed flat-lying sediment. There are, however, areas of the plateau and the surrounding continental slope that show local deformation caused by basement faults, diapirism, slumps, marginal collapse, and cut and fill features. Basement faults, with offsets up to several kilometers, are the major structural features that dominate the Umnak Plateau region. One zone of faults with a cumulative offset of 2 to 3 km is buried beneath the continental slope and parallels the Bering shelf edge. Subsidence across this part of the continental slope has occurred since early Tertiary time (Cooper and others, 1979), however, most of the faults are old features that do not reach the sea floor. Another major basement fault zone may be present along the north side of the Aleutian Ridge (Fig. 17). Here a narrow depression, with a relief of 8 to 9 km, is associated with the fault. An undeformed sedimentary section lies within the depression and abuts against the Aleutian Ridge (Line 1B, Fig. 16). Faults within the sedimentary section occur only at the extreme edge of

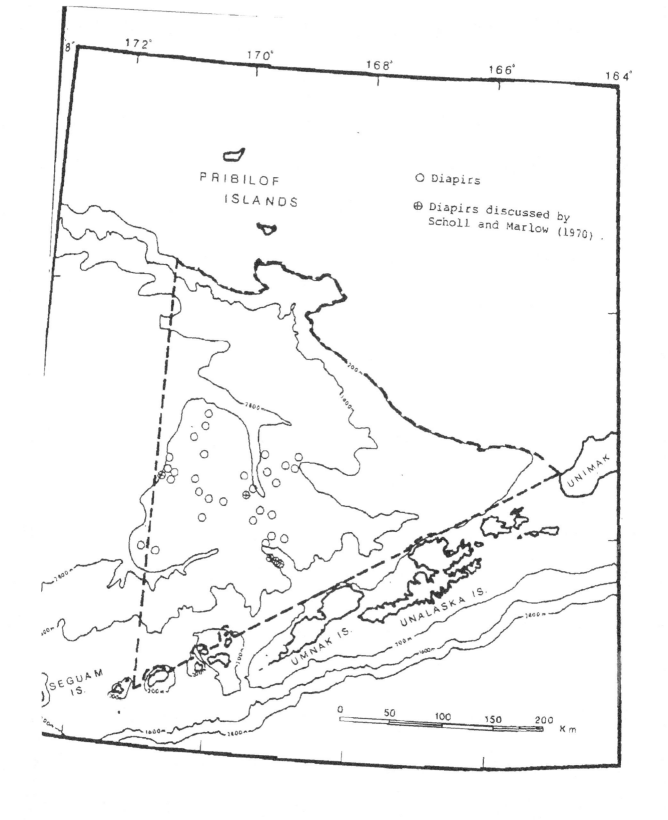

re 21. Map showing the location of diapirs within the Umnak Plateau region.

the depression and do not break the sea floor. Other basement faults under

Umnak Plateau generally trend in the same direction as the fault zones along

both the Aleutian Ridge and the Bering slope and these faults have

displacements of 0.5 to 1.5 km. The initiation of this basement faulting

probably occurred in late Cenozoic time, as evidenced by the uplift and

faulting of late Cenozoic sediment (Fig. 22). Faults within the sedimentary

section beneath the plateau result from either basement faults or local

diapirism, however, faults do not disrupt the sea floor (Fig. 22).

The sedimentary section around the edge of Umnak Plateau is locally

uplifted by underlying basement diapirs or faulted basement blocks (Fig.

22). Based on the continuation of dated horizons from DSDP sites to the

plateau edge, the basement uplifts occurred in late Cenozoic time and prior t

the cutting of the submarine canyons. Above the uplifts, the steep sides of

the canyons are scarred by cut and fill features, and by large bodies of

sediment that have slumped or have collapsed from the edge of the plateau

(Fig. 22). The slumps and collapse structures are features that formed durir

and after the most recent period of canyon cutting.

Submarine Canyons

The three major submarine canyons (Umnak, Bering, Bristol) that disect

the Umnak Plateau region (Fig. 3), are young features that gained their

present configuration during Pliocene-Pleistocene time (Scholl and others,

1970). The course of the canyons appears to be structurally controlled by t

late Cenozoic basement uplifts and diapirs that lie beneath the canyon walls

(Figs. 17, 21). Prior to the canyon cutting, the basement uplifts arched th

overlying sediment and formed small adjacent depressions. These depressions

have been deeply eroded to form the present canyon topography. This phase c

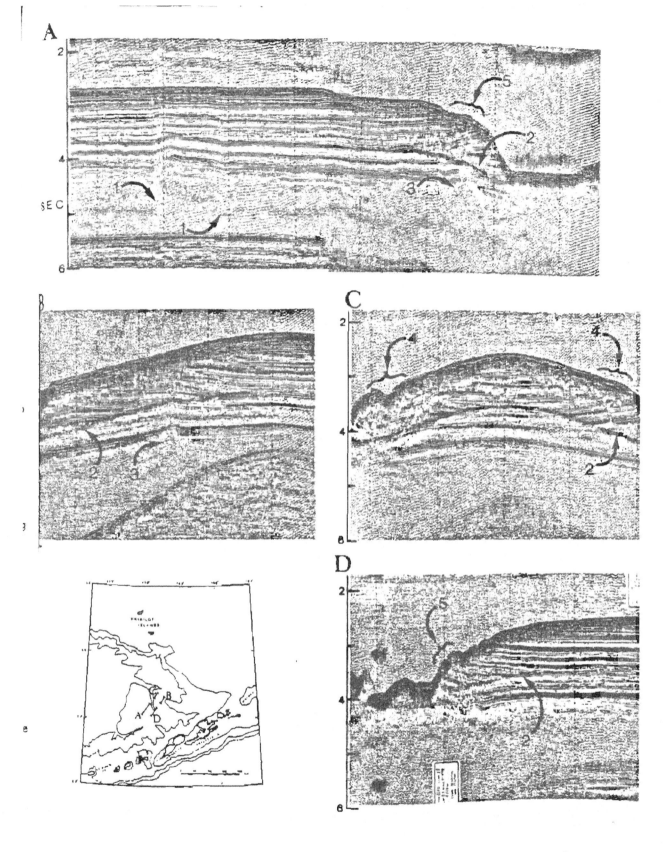

Figure 22.   Seismic reflection profiles across the Umnak Plateau region.
(1) Basement fault, (2) Bottom simulating reflector, (3) Diapir,
(4) Slumps and cut and fill features, (5) Uplifted sedimentary bodies.

The structural framework of the Aleutian Ridge segment that lies within the Umnak Plateau region is incompletely known. The ridge is probably a large antiform constructed mostly by igneous processes. Volcanic and related sedimentary rocks that formed in the summit area of the ridge in early Miocene (or possibly older) time are exposed on Unalaska and Umnak Islands (Fig. 7). These units of the early series are not significantly deformed, although they are thermally altered and intruded by middle Miocene (middle series) granodiorite and gabbro plutons composition (Byers, 1959; Drewes and others, 1961). This framework of marine volcanic and volcanoclastic rocks and associated intrusive masses presumably extends northward beneath the northern flank of the Aleutian Ridge, and possibly in part underlies Umnak Plateau. The construction of the ridge must have begun prior to early Miocene time (before 20-25 m.y.).

Significantly, volcanic rocks of middle Miocene age that are extrusive equivalents of the exposed plutonic bodies have not been mapped on the Aleutian Islands that border the Umnak Plateau region. However, volcanic activity since early Pliocene time (5 m.y ago), has constructed the magnificient stratocones that are distributed in an arcuate array along the crest of the ridge (Fig. 13). The accumulation of these volcanic piles represent the final igneous contributions to the construction of the ridge's structural framework.

44

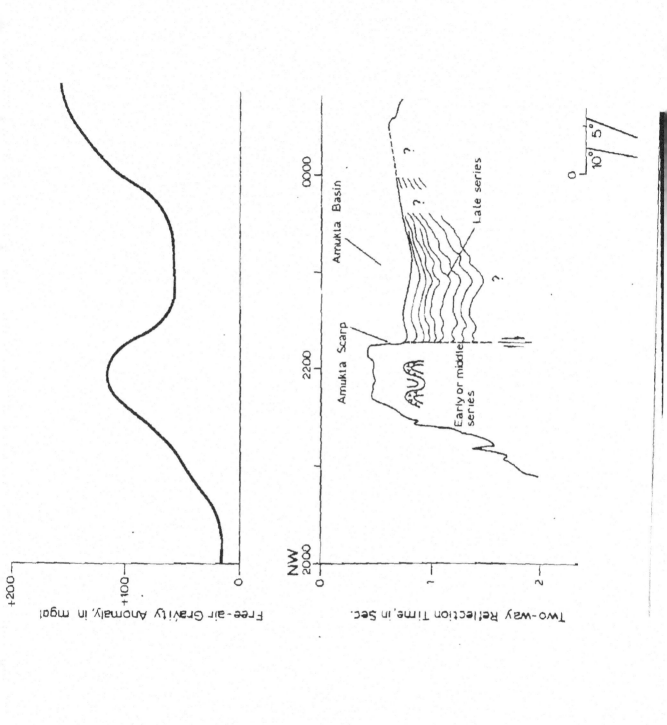

Free-air Gravity Anomaly, in mgal

+200
+100
0

Two-way Reflection Time, in sec.

NW
2000
2200
0000

Amukta Basin

Amukta Scarp

Late series

Early or middle series

?

10°
5°
0

Stratigraphic sequences are also found along the ridge. Within the Umnak
Plateau region, sections of middle and late series sediment underlie the
northern flank of the ridge and fill Amukta Basin (Figs. 10, 11, 23, I). Late
middle series beds beneath the ridge's flank are generally less than 1000-1500
m thick. These slope strata dip northward, parallel to the slope of the ridge
flank, and overlie lithified and thermally altered volcanic and sedimentary
units of the early series (Figs. 10, 11). North of Umnak Island, slope
deposits of early and middle series beds merge with Neogene and younger beds
that underlie Umnak Plateau (Fig. 10). Where these deposits are thicker than
about 1500 m, a bottom simulating reflector (BSR) is characteristically
recorded within the sedimentary section of the ridge's northern flank.

Summit Basins

Sediment beneath the ridge's summit platform represent the middle(?) and
late series which substantially thicken (2-4 km) in summit or perched basins
(Figs. 12, 18, 23; Scholl and others, 1975a). Only a small part of one of
these basins, Amukta Basin, lies within the Umnak Plateau region (Fig. 12).

Amukta Basin, which is structurally contiguous with neighboring Amlia
Basin (Fig. 12), is approximately 4000 km^2 in area (100 x 40 km). Amukta
Basin is elongate parallel to the Aleutian Ridge. The igneous rocks of
several volcanic centers, including those of Amukta, Segram, Carslisle, and
Cajka, may be interbedded with, or intruded into, the sedimentary sequence of
the basin. The northern flank of the basin is bordered by a fault scarp,
Amukta scarp, which is breached by several submarine canyons (Fig. 23).

The formation of Amukta Basin records the beginning of extensional
faulting of the ridge's summit platform. Amukta Basin is largely filled with
sedimentary deposits of the late series (Fig. 23). Cursory

A

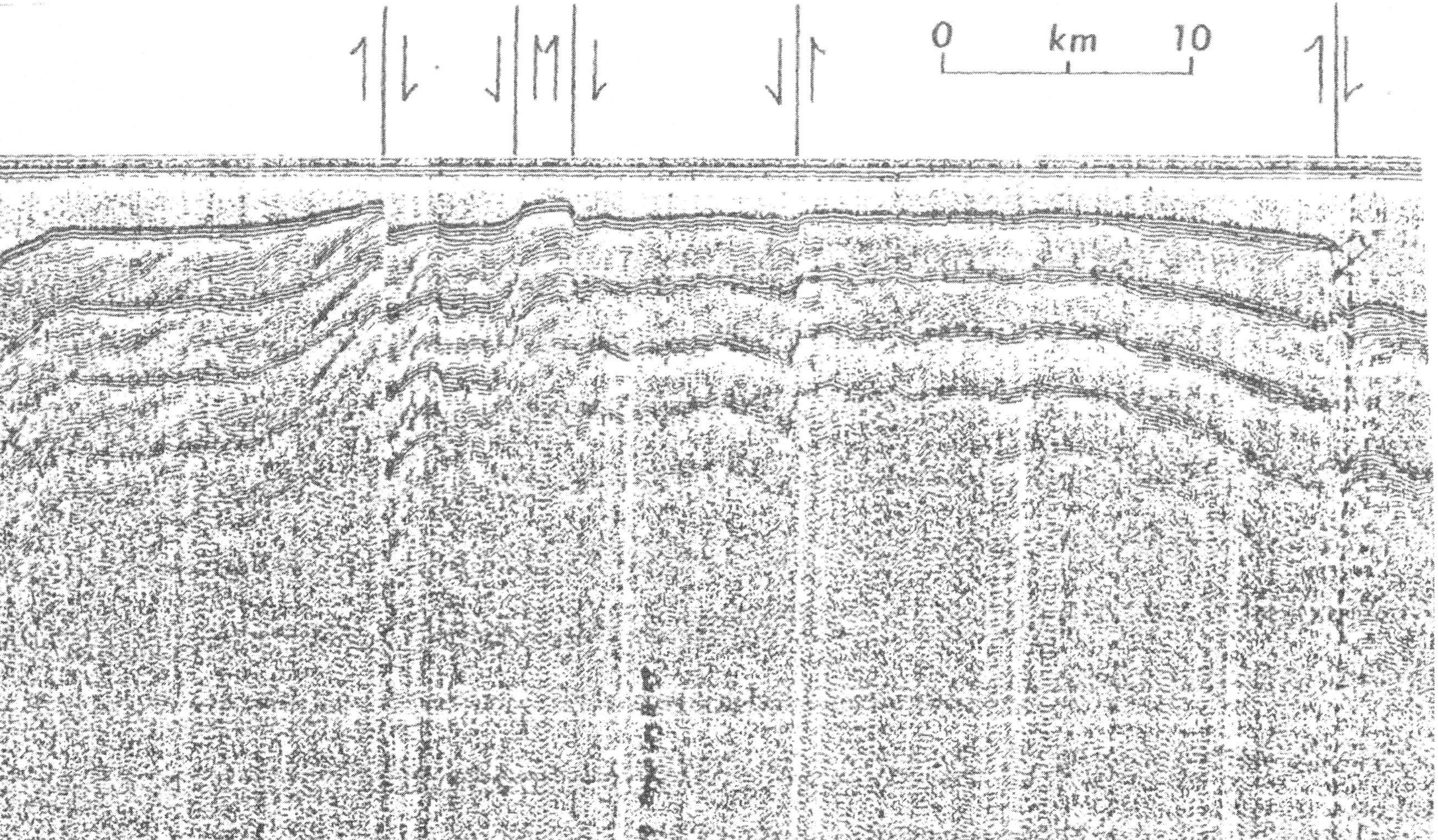

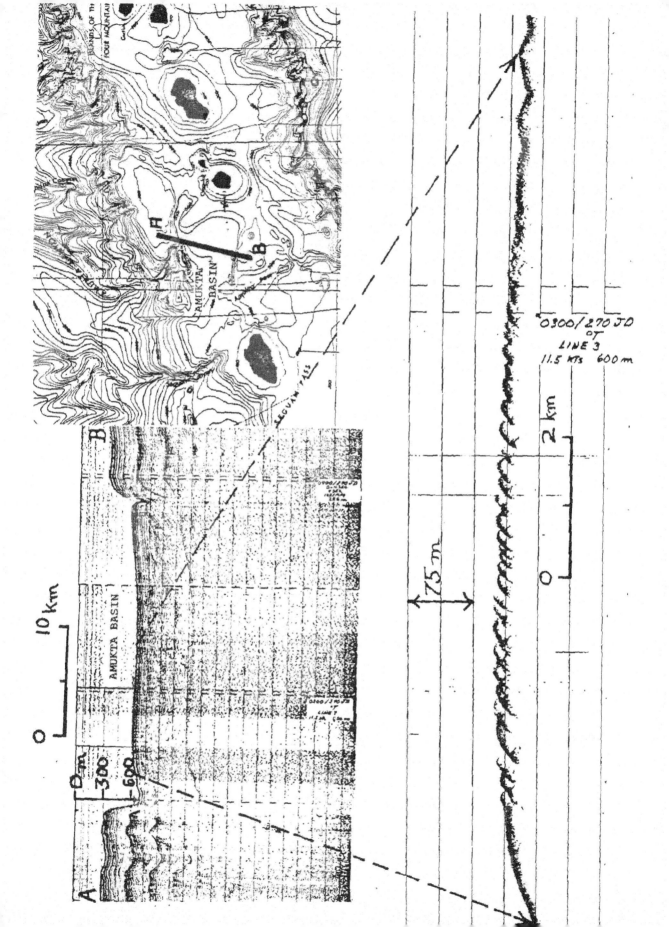

examinations of newly acquired geophysical records (Fig. 24; USGS cruise S6-79-NP) indicate that the late series beds of Amukta Basins are locally folded, and underlie a broader area of the summit platform than realized by Scholl and others (1975a). Also, preliminary examination of samples collected from submarine outcrops imply that middle series beds may also be involved in the basin fill.

Faulting

Late Cenozoic normal faults disrupt the surface of the summit platform and the sedimentary sequences of summit basins (Figs. 24, 25) in the Umnak Plateau region, and elsewhere along the ridge. Faults trend parallel to the axis of the ridge, for example, those that define the northern limits of Amlia and Amukta Basins (Fig. 12), but faults also strike transverse to the ridge's regional trend. Some of the transverse faults control the location and trends of passes and straits that separate the Aleutian Islands.

Geopotential Data

Magnetic Data

The magnetic map for the Umnak Plateau region, (Fig. 26) illustrates the three types of anomalies that characterize the region. The first is a belt of broad positive anomalies that trends north-south across the western half of Umnak Plateau. The second type is a long set of negative anomalies that lie beneath the upper continental slope (adjacent to the 200 m contour) and extend from Pribilof Canyon to the Aleutian Ridge. The third type is a scattering of isolated bullseye anomalies that cover the top and upper flanks of the Aleutian Ridge, the outer Bering shelf, and parts of Umnak Plateau.

In general, the magnetic anomalies over the plateau can be correlated with topographic relief on the acoustic basement (compare Figs. 17 and 26).

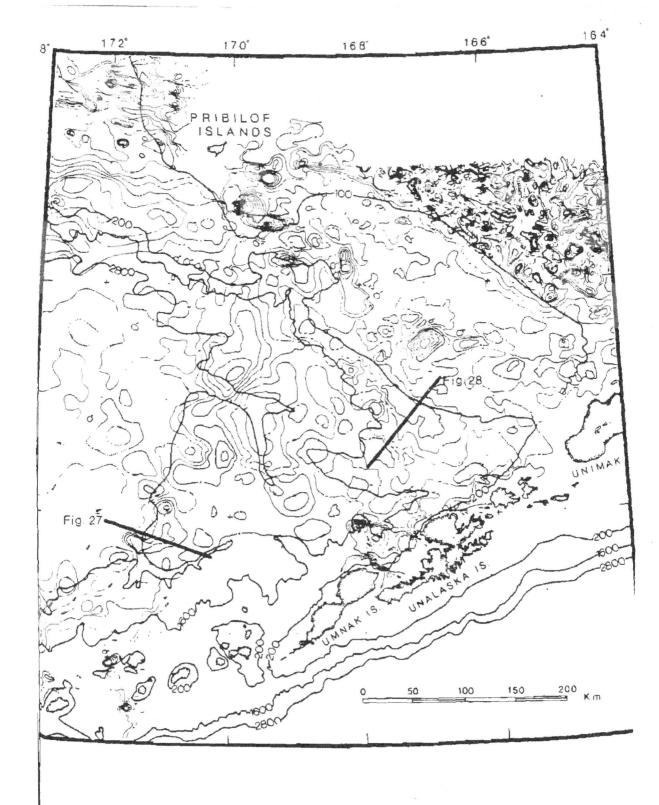

Figure 26. Magnetic map showing residual total field anomalies across the Umnak Plateau region (from Childs and others, in press).

The areas of shallow basement such as the southern and northern parts of Umnak Plateau, have positive magnetic anomalies whereas the deep basement depressions beneath the edge of the continental slope and beneath the central part of Umnak Plateau are characterized by negative anomalies. Bullseye anomalies near the Aleutian Ridge, such as over Bogoslov Island (Fig. 3), are caused by volcanic rocks. Similarly shaped anomalies at the head of Pribilof Canyon are probably caused by volcanic rocks magnetically similar to those found on the Pribilof Islands.

The diapiric intrusions that are seen in the reflection profiles over Umnak Plateau (Fig. 21) are not associated with magnetic anomalies (Scholl and Marlow, 1970); however, small isolated magnetic anomalies are observed over the plateau and these anomalies may be associated with basement ridges. The present physiographic relief of the large submarine canyons does not correlate with the distinctive magnetic anomalies on the map. This observation indicates that the sedimentary section, although rich in volcanic rock fragments (Vallier and others, in press), is not sufficiently magnetic to affect the magnetic anomalies over the canyons where large portions of the sedimentary section have been eroded. Rather, the magnetic anomalies result from magnetic sources that are beneath the sedimentary section.

Magnetic model studies have been constructed from data at two locations. The first model is of the area across the positive anomaly at the outer edge of Umnak Plateau (Fig. 27) and the second is of the region across the negative anomaly beneath the upper continental slope (Fig. 28). The refraction data from the outer edge of the plateau delineate a layer with a velocity typical of the oceanic Layer 2 basalt. If magnetizations typical of basalt are assigned, then the observed magnetic anomaly can be explained as a topographic edge effect of a vertically displaced layer, which may be a piece

51

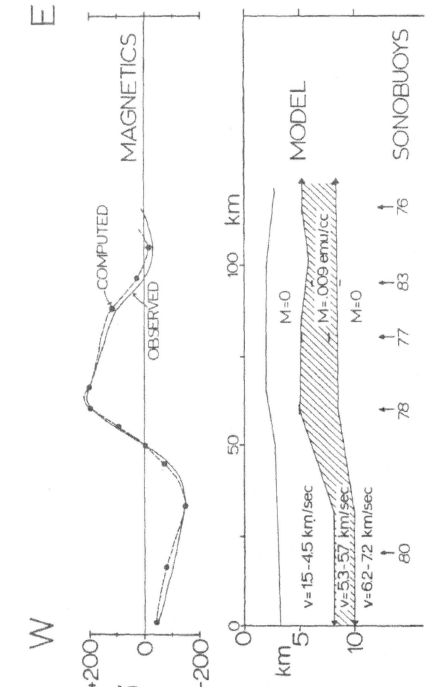

Figure 27. Magnetic model across the western edge of Umnak Plateau. The observed magnetic anomaly may be caused by a segment of uplifted oceanic crust. See figure 26 for location.

SHELF EDGE

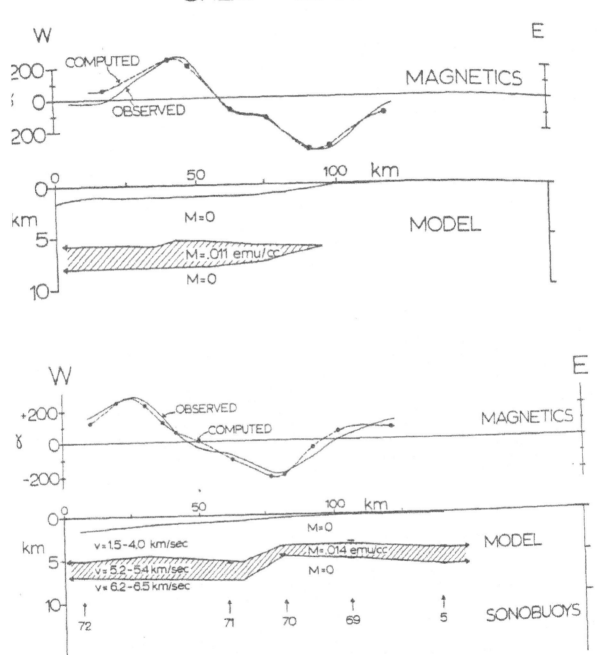

Figure 28. Magnetic model across the edge of the Bering shelf (see figure 26 for location). The observed magnetic anomaly may be caused by a terminated oceanic crust (upper model: based on seismic reflection data) or by a vertically displaced magnetic layer (lower model: based on seismic refraction data). The upper model is prefered.

of uplifted oceanic crust.

Two models can explain the observed negative magnetic anomaly beneath the shelf edge. The first model, in which the top of the magnetic layer is determined from seismic reflection data, depicts a termination of the oceanic crustal layer at the edge of the continental margin. A similar termination of oceanic crust along the Bering margin is reported north of Pribilof Canyon (Cooper and others, 1979a). An alternate model, which is based on the refraction data (Fig. 19), shows a uniformly magnetized layer (flood basalts?) that extends from the shelf out to and over the plateau region. Although the second model is possible, there is no geologic evidence for thick continental flood basalts that may have covered the outer Bering shelf.

The magnetic model studies suggest that Unmak Plateau is underlain by a piece of oceanic crust that has been uplifted and that terminates beneath the upper continental slope.

Gravity Data

The published gravity data over the Umnak Plateau region are sparse and are limited to a map by Watts (1975) and profiles by Marlow and others (1976). A composite map of the gravity data (Fig. 29) indicates that the free-air gravity values are strongly influenced by the large bathymetric relief of the canyons, ridges, and plateaus in the region. The bathymetric highs are associated with large free-air anomalies (25 to 50 mgal) whereas the canyons are characterized by negative anomalies (0 to -25 mgal). The large sediment-filled depression that is buried beneath the upper continental slope (Fig. 17) is associated with a small gravity low (0 to -25 mgal) near the Aleutian Islands and a large low (less than -50 mgal) near Pribilof Canyon. The low near Pribilof Canyon is large, in part, because of the topographic

54

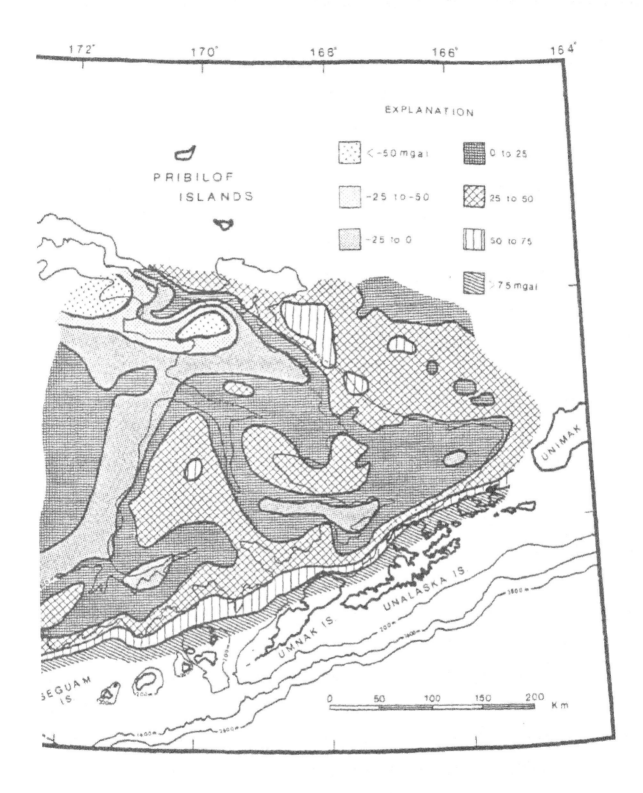

Figure 29. Free-air gravity map of the Umnak Plateau region.

effect of the steep continental slope. Other smaller basement features may be associated with gravity anomalies, however, these features are difficult to identify without the help of gravity modeling studies. The gravimetric effect of the bathymetric features is significantly larger than the gravimetric effect of the basement structures.

The Aleutian ridge is characterized by a 200 to 300 mgal gravity anomaly that parallels the axis of the ridge. A generalized gravity model of the Aleutian Ridge (Grow, 1973) for the area just west of Umnak Plateau region indicates that a stratified density structure within a 20 to 30 km thick crust is necessary to duplicate the observed gravity anomaly. The thick but narrow sedimentary basins that incise the summit of the ridge may have gravity anomalies of -30 to -40 mgal associated with them, as suggested by a gravity profile across Amukta Basin (Fig. 23).

Heat Flow Data

Heat flow measurements have been made at Deep Sea Drilling sites 184 and 185 on Umnak Plateau (Erickson, 1973) and at sites within the Aleutian Basin (Watanabe and others, 1977; Lanseth, pers comm, 1979). The results are sparse (Fig. 30) and the six heat flow values shown on the map cover a wide range from 0.1 to 4.7 HFU (1 HFU=1 ucal/cm^2/sec). The corresponding temperature gradients for each site also vary widely from 6 to 244 °C/km (3 to 134 °F/1000 Ft). If the two extreme heat flow values are excluded, then the remaining four values range from 1.0 to 1.9 HFU and the temperature gradients vary from 50 to 82°C/km (27 to 45°F/1000 Ft). These measurements are reasonable for deep-water marginal basins (Watanabe and others, 1977).

To obtain the actual heat flow values from the region, the observed heat flow values must be corrected for the effect of rapid sedimentation over the

56

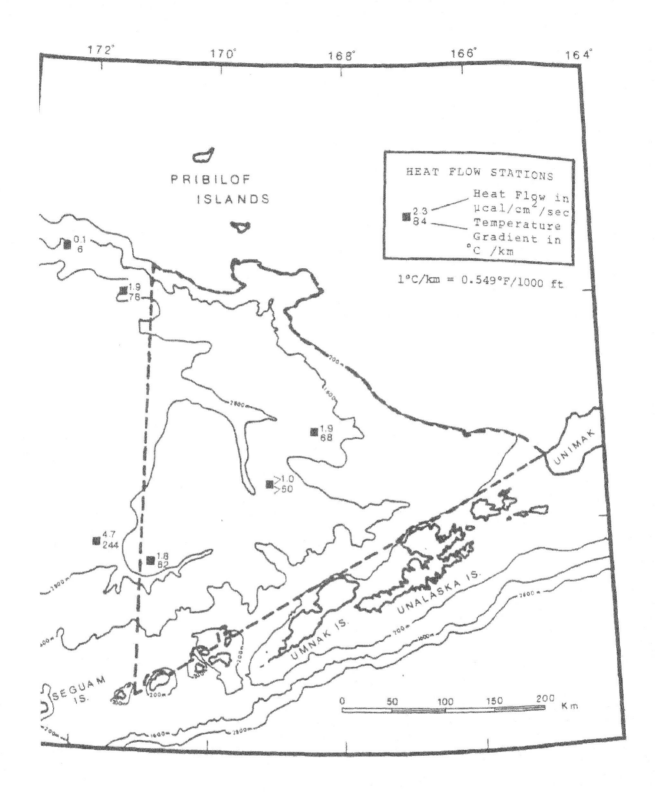

Figure 30. Heat flow stations in the Umnak Plateau region.

plateau. The actual heat flow values (and temperature gradients) will be 20 to 25% higher than the observed values based on sedimentation rates measured at DSDP sites 184 and 185, (Cooper and others, 1977).

The large variation in heat flow values is due to both observational and geologic causes. Minor differences between heat flow values at different stations result from the different instrumental techniques used to measure temperature gradients at the drilling and surface-coring sites as well as from the variation in the amount of sub-surface penetration at the heat flow stations. The geological variations are due in part to regional variations in heat flow at stations located around the volcanically active Aleutian Ridge and to the effects of variable sedimentation rates at each of the heat flow stations.

Regional Synthesis

The offshore geological and geophysical data indicate that the southeast trending belt of Mesozoic rocks exposed on the Alaska Peninsula bends to the northwest and connects with the basement ridges that lie beneath the outer edge of the Bering shelf, west of St. George basin (Marlow and others, 1979a). These Mesozoic rocks are unconformably overlain by shallow-water diatomaceous rocks of early Tertiary age. Mesozoic rocks are not found along the Aleutian Ridge; consequently the ridge is believed to have formed in early Tertiary time (Scholl and others, 1975). The structural framework of the Umnak Plateau region is a complex mixture of the structural histories of both the Mesozoic shelf foldbelt and the Aleutian Ridge island-arc structure.

Umnak Plateau and Continental Slope

The seismic reflection/refraction data and magnetic data provide the best clues to the origin of Umnak Plateau and the continental-slope areas in lieu of deep drilling information. The seismic refraction data indicate the

58

crustal structure beneath the western part of this area is similar to that of oceanic crust whereas the eastern part of the area is underlain by transitional or continental crust. The magnetic data indicate that oceanic Layer 2 (basalt) may extend from the Aleutian Basin to a position under the upper continental slope and that Layer 2 may be uplifted beneath Umnak Plateau.

A model for the evolution of Umnak Plateau (Fig. 31) indicates that until early Tertiary time, the region was underlain by oceanic crust similar to that currently observed in the Aleutian Basin. The location where the oceanic Layer 2 presently terminates beneath the upper continental slope may mark the early Tertiary position for the ocean-continent transition. In early to middle Tertiary time, the oceanic crust and overlying sediment were uplifted and folded into a series of ridges and troughs (Fig. 17). The uplift may have been in response to the compressional forces generated by the large change in underthrusting direction of the Pacific plate beneath the Aleutian Ridge that occurred at this time. The flat-lying sequence of terrigenous and diatomaceous sediment that blankets the entire Umnak Plateau region has been deposited since this period of uplift. The rapid infilling of troughs and accumulation of a thick sedimentary section after the uplift probably resulted in differential loading that deformed the old layer of uplifted sediment. This old layer, may be the acoustically opaque high-velocity layer that now lies between acoustic basement and the underlying igneous crustal rocks. This layer may be a mobil shale unit that could be the source for the diapirs that have pierced the sedimentary section since middle to late Miocene time. Erosion of the three major submarine canyons that disect the region may have occurred throughout Cenozoic Time, however, the present physiography of the canyons is the result of Pliocene to Pleistocene erosion. The trend of the

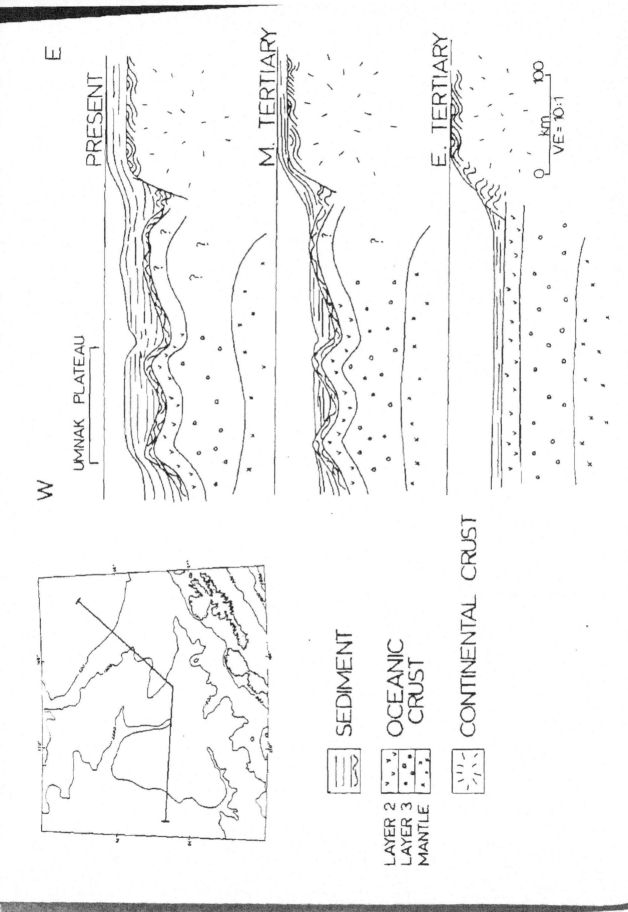

Figure 31. Model for the evolution of Umnak Plateau and nearby areas.

canyons may have been controlled by the ancient sea floor topography that was

caused by diapiric uplift of the sedimentary section.

The same period that crustal uplift, sedimentation, and diapiric

processes affected the western part of the Umnak Plateau region, rapid

subsidence and sediment infill occurred in the eastern part of the region.

The subsidence and collapse of the outer Bering shelf that has been documented

north of Pribilof Canyon (Cooper and others, 1979) also occurred in the Umnak

Plateau region. The collapse resulted in the formation of the deep structural

depressions that lie along the upper continental slope and along the north

side of the Aleutian Ridge.

Aleutian Ridge

The initial formation of the Aleutian Ridge by either tectonic or

magmatic process is ascribed to the fragmentation of the Kula plate, which, in

late Cretaceous time (70 m.y. ago), occupied the far north Pacific area

(Scholl and others, 1975a; Cooper and others, 1976). By middle to late Eocene

time (45-38 m.y.), igneous processes had constructed the bulk of the Aleutian

Ridge and subaerial volcanic masses were common. Prior to about 25 m.y.

virtually all the volcanic rocks of the ridge were thermally altered (DeLong

ind McDowell, 1975), although associated sedimentary masses were less

:hermally altered but rather broadly folded or flexed. An important episode

f igneous activity affected the Aleutian Ridge in middle Miocene time (15-10

.y.), and contributed to the further alteration of older sedimentary volcanic

isses. During middle and late Miocene time (15-5 m.y.), regional erosion of

ie summit area of the ridge by subaerial and coastal processes carved the

.dge's prominent summit platform. Extensional rifting and differential

bsidence of this platform began approximately 5-10 m.y. ago, apparently in conjunction with the outbreak of explosive volcanism that formed the lofty volcanoes of the arcuate Aleutian chain. Debris eroded from the crestal area of the ridge has accumulated as thick slope deposits on the flanks of the ridge and also in the summit basins.

The geologic history of the Aleutian Ridge during the past 40-50 m.y. is a record of the interactions of the Pacific and North American plates. The relative direction and speed of these interactions may have changed with time, and thereby determined the course of the igneous, structural, and sedimentological evolution of the ridge.

PETROLEUM GEOLOGY

Umnak Plateau and Continental Slope

The petroleum geology of the areas surrounding the Umnak Plateau region
have been discussed by Marlow and others (1979a; Alaska Peninsula and Bering
shelf) and by Cooper and others (1979; Aleutian Basin). Since only two
shallow wells have been drilled on Umnak Plateau the information about deeply-
buried source and reservoir beds must be derived from rocks dredged from the
continental slope. In the following sections each of the four requisites for
hydrocarbon generation and accumulation are discussed: source beds,
reservoirs, traps, thermal and sedimentation history.

Source Beds

The average organic carbon value for 85 rock samples obtained from DSDP
drilling (Bode, 1973; Underwood and others, 1979) and from dredging (Marlow
and others, 1976, 1979b; Underwood and others, 1979) in the Umnak Plateau
region is 0.5 $\pm$ 0.21%. Nearly 60% of these samples are from the late Miocene
to Holocene diatomaceous siltstones recovered at DSDP sites 184 and 185 and
the other samples are from the middle to late Miocene age diatomaceous rocks
dredged in the Pribilof Canyon. Four samples of Cretaceous mudstone from
Pribilof Canyon have as much as 1% organic carbon but the average for the four
samples is 0.62%.

The middle Miocene and younger mudstones that have been dredged from the
continental slope are from the upper part of the sedimentary sequence that
blankets the Umnak Plateau region. The organic carbon content of these fine-
grained mudstones may be representative of other more deeply buried mudstones
beneath the region; three Paleogene dredge samples have an average organic
carbon content of 0.5% (Marlow and others, 1976, 1979b).

The average organic carbon content (0.5%) of the dredge samples from Umnak Plateau region indicates that adequate source beds could be present within the 3 to 8 km thick sedimentary section.

Reservoir Beds

Combined porosity and permeability measurements have been made on onl few Tertiary rocks dredged from the Bering slope (Marlow and others, 1979a and on Pliocene diatomaceous sediment recovered from DSDP Sites 188 and 19(the Bowers and Aleutian Basins (Cooper and others, 1979). Porosity measurements have been reported for the Miocene to Holocene sedimentary sections at DSDP Sites 184 and 185 on Umnak Plateau (Creager and others, 1973), and for other dredge samples along the Bering slope (Marlow and othe 1976).

The porosity of the diatomaceous oozes and siltstone in the upper 600 meters of the sedimentary section at DSDP Sites 184 and 185 ranges from 60 t 80%. A sharp decrease in porosity from 75 to 40% occurs at a depth of 600 to 650 meters across a diagenetic boundary between overlying oozes and underlyi mudstone (Lee, 1973). Porosities of mid-Oligocene to late Miocene rocks dredged from the Bering slope fall into two porosity ranges; mudstone, siltstone, and tuffs range from 45% to 68% and calcareous argillite and lithi wackes range from 14 to 29%. The data demonstrate that highly porous horizon may be found throughout the sedimentary section.

Only four permeability values have been reported for the dredge samples from the along the Bering slope and these values (5, 1, 19, 2 mdarcy) are for late Oligocene to middle Miocene mudstone, siltsone, and tuffs. Cooper and others (1979) discuss the permeability of diatomaceous sediment with porosities and diatom contents that are similar to those found under Umnak

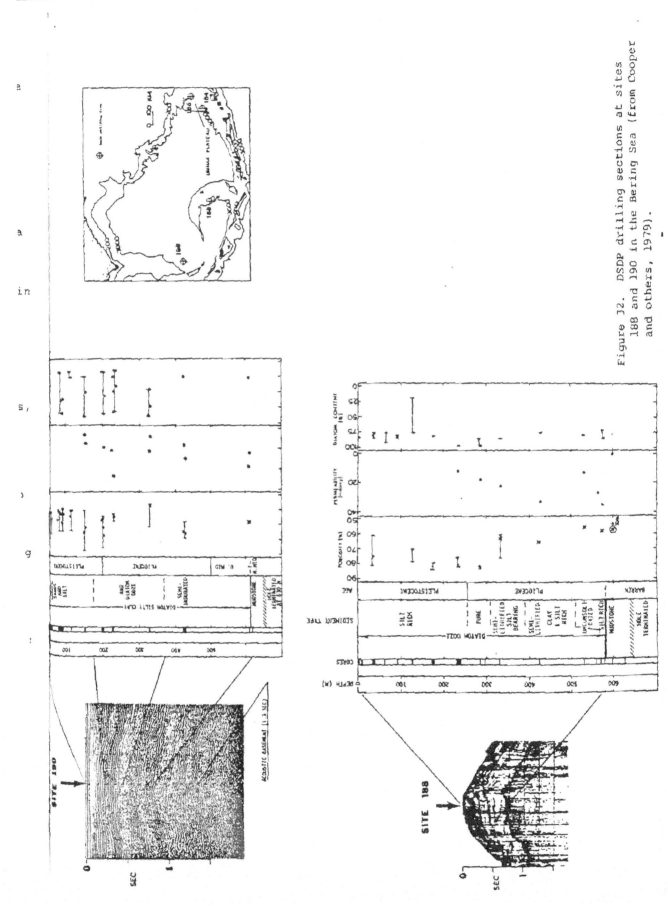

Figure 32. DSDP drilling sections at sites 188 and 190 in the Bering Sea (from Cooper and others, 1979).

Plateau (Fig. 32). They note that the permeabilities of diatoms are large (6 to 49 mdarcy), permeability increases with depth from about 10 mdarcy at 150 meters depth to about 30 mdarcy at 600 meters depth and permeabilities decrease from 35 to .01 mdarcy across the diagenetic boundary between oozes and mudstone. The sedimentary sections on Umnak Plateau contain a larger volcanogenic and terrigenous component than the two sites studied by Cooper and others (1979) hence the permeability values may differ in the two areas.

The degree of diagenesis and lithification within the sedimentary section, especially at the diagenetic boundary between the diatomaceous oozes and indurated mudstone, has had a significant effect on the permeability and the porosity of potential reservoir beds. The areal distribution of the diagenetic boundary is an important factor that may limit the regional extent of reservoir beds that may exist in the thick Tertiary sedimentary section. High porosities (45 to 80%) and potentially good permeabilities (Cooper and others, 1979), however, are favorable indicators that potential reservoir units for the accumulation of hydrocarbons may exist in the upper 600 meters of the sedimentary section. These favorable indicators also exist in adjacent areas of the Aleutian Basin (Cooper and others, 1979).

Seals

A mechanism for the trapping and accumulation of hydrocarbons within the porous diatomaceous sediment sections of abyssal basins has been proposed for the Aleutian Basin (Cooper and others, 1979) and the Sea of Japan (Schlanger and Combs, 1975). These models allow hydrocarbons to be stored within a porous diatomaceous sedimentary section that is sandwiched between underlying mudstone and overlying turbidites. The turbidite unit is the stratigraphic seal that caps the diatomaceous reservoir unit. In the Aleutian Basin, Figure

65

velocity-amplitude features (VAMPs), which are acoustic features indicative of gas-charged sediment (Fig. 33), are found at the base of the turbidite unit.

A similar mechanism for the accumulation of hydrocarbons may be possible for parts, but not all, of the Umnak Plateau region. Although the underlying mudstone and the diatomaceous sediment are present, the capping turbidite layer may only be present at the base of Umnak Plateau and in the floors and overbank deposits of the submarine canyons. If hydrocarbons are being generated within deeply buried mudstone beds, then other seals, such as an impermeable layer of altered volcanic sediment or an overlying clathrate layer must be present. Preliminary inspection of the seismic reflection records indicates that the turbidite seals that probably exist in the Aleutian Basin may not be present in the Umnak Plateau region. Only one VAMP has been found in the region and this VAMP ws observed beneath the flat-lying sediment section of the upper continental slope.

Diagenetic Boundary - Bottom Simulating Reflector (BSR)

The diagenetic boundary that occurs at a sub-bottom depth of 600 meters, and that causes a prominent reflection horizon (BSR) beneath most of the Umnak Plateau region may play an important role in the distribution of any hydrocarbons that may exist in the region:

- The boundary is believed to represent an isothermal surface (Bein and
    others, 1978) that cuts across stratigraphic time horizons and
    affects all Tertiary diatomaceous rocks.

- A major change occurs in the lithology and physical properties (porosity,
    permeability, density, acoustic velocity) of the sediment across the
    boundary. These changes that can affect the flow of fluids/gases
    across the boundary.

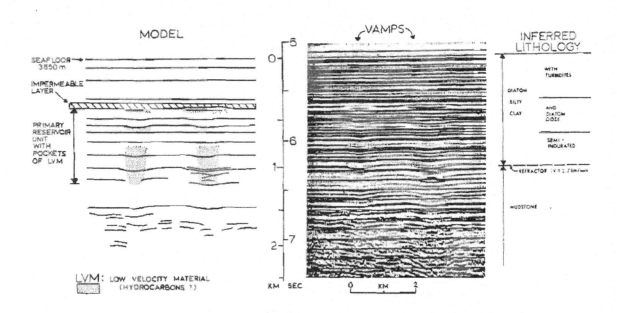

Figure 33. Model explaining the occurrence of VAMPs (from Cooper and others, 1979).

- The boundary is associated with higher than normal concentrations of

    methane gas at Site 185 but is not associated with gas at Site 184.

    This gas may be a biproduct of the diagenetic process (Hein and

    others, 1978) or may be biogenic/thermogenic gas trapped within the

    thin diagenetic zone.

- The boundary may be a nearly impermeable barrier that controls the

    trapping or channeling of migrating hydrocarbons in areas where

    sediment is faulted or folded, such as along the sides of the

    submarine canyons, along the continental slope, and above diapiric

    intrusions on Umnak Plateau.

Traps

Structural and stratigraphic traps may be present throughout the Umnak

Plateau region. Structures such as diapirs, uplifted sedimentary bodies, and

buried faults (Fig. 22) are common and may be associated with hydrocarbon

traps. The deep sediment-filled depressions beneath the upper continental

slope and the north side of the Aleutian Ridge (Fig. 17) are presumed to be

bounded by deeply buried faults. These deep faults do not break the sea floor

but they may provide sub-surface routes along which fluids/gases can migrate

upward from deeply buried sources. Some basement uplifts beneath Umnak

Plateau are fault bounded. These basement faults fracture deep sediment

layers and deform the overlying sediment horizons (Fig. 22A). The folded and

uplifted sediment that is associated with the basement faults is a potential

hydrocarbon trap. Cooper and others (1979) discuss other examples of

structural traps that are found in nearby areas of the Aleutian Basin and

continental slope.

Stratigraphic features such as pinchouts, filled channels, lateral

69

diagenetic variations, and buried slumps are common and may also trap hydrocarbons. These features are all found beneath the continental slope, although they are more common in the canyon-scarred areas of the slope. The lateral diagenetic variations beneath Umnak Plateau, may, however, be the most important stratigraphic trapping mechanism. Pinchouts are common in all areas of the Umnak Plateau region where the sedimentary section has undergone rapid vertical displacement. Pinchouts are observed above structural depressions beneath the continental slope (Fig. 16), over basement warps beneath Umnak Plateau (Figs. 16, 22), and near diapiric intrusions at the edge of Umnak Plateau (Fig. 22). Old filled channels found near the edge of the present submarine canyons are depositional features that formed during the Late Cenozoic period of canyon cutting. These features may be of limited importance in the accumulation of hydrocarbons because they are relatively young..

Thermal History

The hydrocarbon potential of a sedimentary sequence such as that found beneath the Umnak Plateau region is largely dependent upon the length of time that the sedimentary sequence has been exposed to the high burial temperatures necessary for the kerogen-hydrocarbon transformation (Schlanger and Combs, 1975). The observed temperature gradients in the Umnak Plateau region are large (50 to 82°C/km or 27 to 45°F/1000 ft, Fig. 30) possibly because of the proximity to the Aleutian Ridge. Similar temperature gradients have probably existed throughout Cenozoic Time as a consequence of episodic magmatic activity along the Aleutian Ridge. If the observed gradients are projected downward, then the onset temperatures for hydrocarbon generation (50 to 100°C) will be reached at relatively shallow sub-bottom depths (0.6 to 2.0 km). The

ENVIRONMENTAL HAZARDS

Potential environmental hazards in the ddep water areas of proposed OCS
Lease Sale 70 have not been thoroughly evaluated. This part of the report,
therefore, is necessarily a cursory review of potential hazards and is based
on the regional geologic setting of the area and on preliminary studies of
singe-channel seismic reflection profiles. We can speculate that several
geologic processes can affect petroleum exploration and production in the
area, but we strongly caution that much more data are needed for even a
preliminary asessment of potential environmental hazards.

The major potential geologic hazards are 1) volcanic activity, 2)
seismicity, 3) active faulting, 4) submarine slumping, 5) current- and wave-
induced sediment transport, and 6) diapirism. Minor hazards such as shoreline
effects by storm waves and landsliding can be locally important.

Volcanic Activity

Studies of the Aleutian Islands volcanoes have been conducted since the
early work by Robinson (1947). Coats (1950) reports that the Aleutian Islands
have at least 76 major volcanic centers and that 36 of these have been active
since 1760. All of the islands have volcanic origins and, within the area of
this report, 23 have been identified of which 14 are active (Fig. 13; Table
1). Most volcanoes lie along the axis of the Aleutian Ridge, but Bogoslof
(Byers, 1959) lies about 40 km north of Umnak Island.

Aleutian volcanoes erupt lavas that typically have high silica contents
and high viscosities. This type of volcano can be highly explosive. Several
Aleutian volcanoes outside of the Umnak Plateau region have explosively and
catastrophically erupted during the past 10,000 years; Fisher Caldera on
Unimak Island, Akutan volcano on Akutan Island, Mt. Makushin on Unalaska
Island, and Okmok Caldera on Umnak Island (Byers, 1959) have violently

exploded in the Holocene (Miller and Barnes, 1976). Investigations of these volcanoes are presently underway (Miller and Smith, 1977).

Since historic records of cataclysmic eruptions in the Umnak Plateau are not available, we cannot effectively evaluate the potential hazards of these great volcanoes. Some of the violent eruptions were probably similar to the eruption at Krakatau in 1883. If any facilities are sited near one of these volcanoes, the potential risk should be carefully evaluated. In 1944, for example, a spectacular eruption of Okmok volcano on Unmak Island nearly caused the evacuation of a military airbase (Robinson, 1947).

Seismicity

The southern boundary of the Umnak Plateau region falls within the Aleutian seismic zone, one of the most active zones in the world (Fig. 34). Numerous papers describing the general aspects of this seismic zone in terms of earthquake frequency, hypocentral depth, magnitude, and mechanism have been published on the Aleutian area since the early 1950's. However, only during the past decade, after completion of the World Seismic Network and atomic testing at Amchitka Island, and in response to increased interest in earthquake prediction, have detailed examinations of the Aleutian seismic zone been possible. The salient results of most of these investigations are reported by Davies and House (1979).

The belt of epicenters that falls along the southern part of the Umnak Plateau region follows the arcuate geometry of the Aleutian Ridge (Fig. 34). The width of the belt, measured normal to the arc, is approximately 300 km. The number of earthquakes apparently is lowest near the base of the ridge's northern and southern slopes, and highest beneath the crestal area of the ridge.

Earthquakes in the Umnak Plateau region occur at increasingly greater

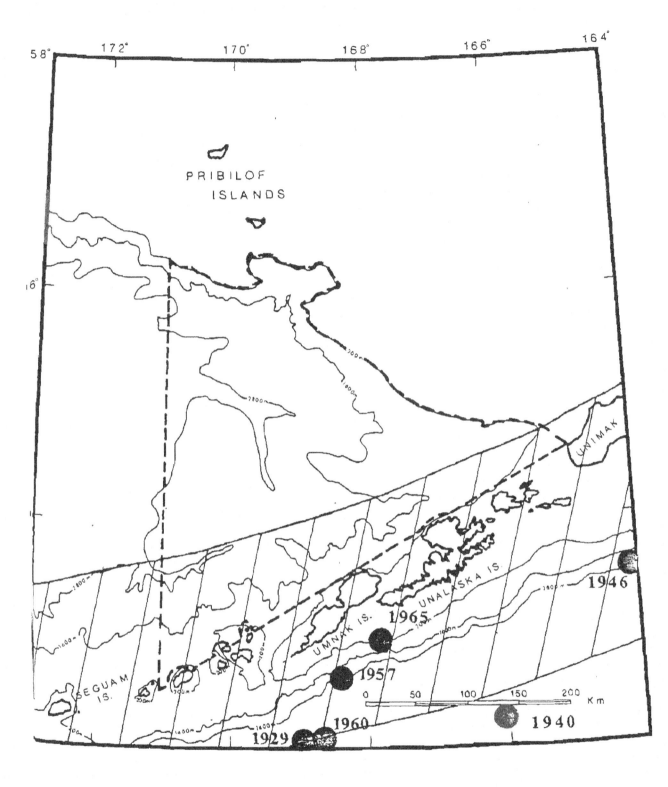

Figure 34. Seismicity of the Aleutian Ridge. Ruled areas show approximate
limits of the Aleutian seismic zone. Large dots are approximate locations of great earthquakes (magnitude larger than 7.0) listed by
Sykes (1971).

depth with distance north of the frontal or Pacific slope of the ridge. The
northward-inclined zone of seismicity, the Benioff Zone, begins at a
subsurface depth of approximately 40 km beneath the southern edge of the
summit platform. The distribution of hypocenters above 40 km is more diffuse;
recent analyses by Davis and House (1979) established that the inclined
Benioff seismic zone is about 10 km thick, and, in the Umnak Plateau region,
the dip of the zone is about 45°-50°. The Benioff zone lies approximately 95
km below the arcuate array of the Aleutian volcanoes.

Earthquakes pose three distinct geohazards in the Umnak Plateau region:
(1) severe ground shaking caused by a great earthquake (magnitude greater than
7; Sykes, 1971), (2) frequent earthquakes of low to moderate magnitude that
may be associated with progressive rupturing of the sea floor, and (3)
tsunamis or seismic sea waves. Great earthquakes, and their destructive
potential in terms of violent ground motion and associated tsunamis, occur
commonly in the vicinity of the Umnak Plateau region. At least 16 great
earthquakes have occurred along the Aleutian seismic zone since 1929 (Sykes,
1971). Six of these quakes, with magnitudes varying from 7.0 to 8.6, occurred
along or adjacent to the southern part of the Umnak Plateau region (Fig.
34). One of these quakes, the 1946 shock seaward of Unimak Island, generated
one of the most destructive tsunamis recorded in the Pacific (Sykes, 1971).
Davies and House (1979) emphasize that the Shumagin Island region immediately
east of the southeast corner of the lease area has been identified as a
seismic gap, which is a section of the Aleutian seismic zone that has not been
ruptured by a great earthquake within the past 20 to 30 years. This
circumstance predicts the likelihood that a potentially destructive and
possibly tsunami-generating earthquake will occur close to the Umnak Plateau
region within the next few decades.

Seismic reflection profiles commonly reveal fault scarps cutting the Aleutian Ridge summit platform and sloping flanks. Epicenteral information is presently too meager to determine if low and moderate magnitude earthquakes are associated with these scarps, but the inference that a relationship seems likely.

Active Faulting

Numerous scarps, some as high as 150m, rupture the planar surface of the Aleutian Ridge summit platform (Fig. 25). These scarps apparently are fault-controlled because they border summit basins, disrupt the basin's sedimentary fill, and determine the locations of inter-island passes and straits. The stress pattern and rate of faulting recorded by the scarps are unknown. Not even the length of these scarps is known. Fault length is an important factor because length can be related to the magnitude of earthquakes associated with the faults. It is reasonable to assume that the faults are presently active because many of the scarps are well expressed geomorphically.

Little is known about active faulting on the northern flank of the ridge. The occurrence of active volcanism and regional seismicity imply that the upper or shallow-water part of the ridge flank is probably affected by surface rupturing. Surface faults have been observed in seismic-reflection profiles from parts of Umnak Plateau and the continental slope along the eastern part of the area, but detailed mapping has not been attempted. The lengths, offsets, and types of slope faults are unknown. Many of the faults are commonly associated with large slumps.

Submarine Slumps

Many areas along the slopes of Umnak Plateau and below the shelf break along the continental margin and Aleutian Ridge are marked by scars and hummocky topography that most likely are related to submarine slumping.

Detached sediment bodies are common in the steep areas, especially along submarine canyon walls, and sediment creep is observed along the more gentle slopes between the Pribilof and Being submarine canyons. Similar bodies and effects are common on seismic-reflection profiles across margins of Umnak Plateau. The areas of greatest slump potential are those that have thick sequences of semi-consolidated middle and late series beds (MLS sequence) and steep slopes.

Sediment Transport

Tide-generated currents as swift as 9 to 10 knots sweep through narrow passes between islands along the Aleutian Ridge. These currents are swift enough to move coarse grained sediments and to generate moving bedforms.

Seismic-reflection profiles taken across Amukta basin reveal bedforms that imply swift currents also exist in deeper water areas (Fig. 24). Here, the bedforms appear to be large (10 x 200 m to 10 x 1000 m) sediment waves. These bedforms may be presently active or moving. An alternative explanation is that they are relict features, possibly formed in lower sea level regimes during the last glaciation. Sediment, therefore, is moved rapidly in tide-dominated shallow-water passes, as well as in other areas of the summit platform. The rate of sediment transport, the net direction of transport, and the volume of debris being transported, are virtually unknown factors for most areas of the summit platform and its flanking slopes.

Part of the sediment that sweeps through the passes may be deposited in the submarine canyons that cut the north flank of the Aleutian Ridge. Turbidity currents and debris flows associated with the mass movement of this sediment would be transported down the submarine canyons and out onto the floor of the Aleutian Basin.

The effects of wave erosion, wave transport, and longshore currents als have not been evaluated. We suspect that the irregularities of the shoreline plus the frequency and strengths of the storms in the area produce significant erosion and transport of sediment.

Diapirism

Numerous diapirs of probable sedimentary origin are found on Umnak Plateau and along the north flank of the Aleutian Ridge (Fig. 21). The origin of the diapirs on Umnak Plateau may be the injection of a mobile shale unit into the sedimentary section. Hence, overpressured shale units may be present in the area of diapirs, a potential hazard to drilling operations.

HYDROCARBON RESOURCE ASSESSMENT

Umnak Plateau region covers the southern and deep-water part of lease sale area #70 (Fig. 2). The assessment of hydrocarbon resources given herein applies to all areas of this region. A large summit basin of the Aleutian Ridge, Amukta Basin, lies immediately adjacent to the southwestern edge of the Umnak Plateau region. A hydrocarbon assessment of this outlying summit basin, one of many, has not been made, yet the existence of these summit basins should be noted for future resource appraisals.

Negligible amounts of undiscovered-recoverable oil and gas are estimated to be present in the Umnak Plateau region. Quantities of undiscovered recoverable oil and gas, as assessed here, are defined as those quantities that are recoverable at current cost and price relationships and at current technology, assuming an additional natural short-term technologic growth.

A review of the geology of the area indicates that potential source beds and a thermal gradient adequate for hydrocarbon generation may be present. Several diapiric structures of unknown trapping potential are also mapped. However, the possibility of adequate reservoir beds is considered to be poor. The sedimentary section is described as consisting of fine-grained mudstone, siltstone and diatomaceous ooze that were deposited in a deep water slope and bathyal environment.

Porosities and permeabilities, previously described in this report, were measured for diatomaceous ooze and siltstone and it is suggested that there is marked decrease in these potential reservoir qualities at a depth of 600-650 meters. There is no indication of the presence of coarse grained sediment that might be suitable for adequate hydrocarbon reservoirs.

The deep-water factor was also dominent in the assessment of neglible amounts of undiscovered recoverable hydrocarbons. About 19,500 mi^2 (50,506

82

km^2) or 62% of the total area lies in water depths greater than 1,600 m (5,240 ft) and 6550 mi^2 (18,965 km^2) or 20% of the total area is in water depths greater than 2,500 m (8,200 ft).

Careful consideration of the probably unfavorable reservoir conditions combined with the more definitely unfavorable condition of water depth led to the assessment of negligible amounts of undiscovered-recoverable oil and gas resources. However, hydrocarbons may exist here in settings which possible could be productive in the distant future under different conditions of economy and technology.

Additional geologic and geophysical information will be required in the future to accurately update assessments of the hydrocarbon potential of the Umnak Plateau region.

Acknowledgements

We would like to thank our U. S. Geological Survey colleagues Mike
Marlow, Jim Gardner, Jon Childs, and Gordon Dolton for helpful discussions
relating to the geology, structure, and petroleum potential of the Umnak
Plateau region. Jim Gardner kindly provided unpublished seismic reflection
data and a diapir map from Umnak Plateau. Jon Childs has been instrumental in
the analysis of seismic sonobuoy data and kindly provided unpublished figures
from his 1979 AGU talk; Jon also provided the computer expertise required for
the compilation of many figures in the text. The neat and timely presentation
of this report would not have been possible without the creative drafting
talents of David Jones and Sue McGeary as well as the consistantly accurate
work of Dorothy Sicard in handling the word processing computer.

REFERENCES

Beikman, H., 1978, Preliminary geologic map of Alaska: U.S. Geological Survey
    Map, 2 sheets, scale 1:2,500,000.

Bode, G.W., 1973, Carbon-Carbonate, in Creager, J.S., ed., and others, Initial
    reports of the Deep Sea Drilling Project, v. 19: Washington, D.C., U.S.
    Government Printing Office, p. 663-666.

Byers, F.M., Jr., 1959, Geology of Umnak and Bogoslof Islands, Alaska: U.S.
    Geology Survey Bull. 1028-L, p. 267-369.

Carr, W.J., Quinlivan, W.D., and Gard, L.M., Jr., 1970, Age and stratigraphic
    relations of Amchitka, Banjo Point, and Chitka Point Formations, Amchitka
    Island, Aleutian Islands, Alaska, in Changes in stratigraphic
    nomenclature by the U.S. Geological Survey, 1969: U.S. Geological Survey
    Bull. 1324-A, p. A16-A22.

Carr, W.J., Gard, L.M., Bath, G.D., and Healey, D.L., 1971, Earth-science
    studies of a nuclear test area in the western Aleutian Islands, Alaska:
    an interim summary of result: Geol. Soc. America Bull., v. 82, p. 699-
    706.

Childs, J.R., and Cooper, A.K., 1979, Marine seismic sonobuoy data from the
    Bering Sea region: U.S. Geol. Survey Open-File Rept. OF79-371.

Childs, J.R., Cooper, A.K., and Parker, A.W., 1979a, Sonobuoy Studies of Umnak
    Plateau, Bering Sea (abs.): EOS (Am. Geophys. Union Trans.) Vol. 60, No.
    18, p. 390.

Coats, R.R., 1950, Volcanic activity in the Aleutian arc: U.S. Geol. Survey
    Bull., 974-B, p. 35-49.

Coats, R.R., 1956a, Geology of northern Adak Island: U.S. Geol. Survey Bull.
    1028-C, p. 45-67.

Coats, R.R., 1956b, Reconnaissance geology of some western Aleutian Islands,
    Alaska: U.S. Geol. Survey Bull. 1028-O, p. 477-519

Cooper, A.K., Scholl, D.W., and Marlow, M.S., 1976, Plate tectonic model for
-    the evolution of the eastern Bering Sea Basin: Geol. Soc. America Bull.,
    v. 87, p. 1119-1126.

Cooper, A.K. Marlow, M.S., and Scholl, D.S., 1977, The Bering Sea - A
    multifarious marginal basin, in Island arcs, deep sea trenches, and back-
    arc basins, v. 1: Am. Geophys. Union, p. 436-450.

Cooper, A.K., Marlow, M.S., and Scholl, D.W., 1979, Thick sediment
    accumulations beneath continental margin of outer Bering Sea (abs):
    AAPG-SEPN program, Annual Convention, April 1979, p. 72.

Cooper, A.K., Marlow, M.S., Parker, A.W., Childs, J.R., 1979, Structure-
    contour map on acoustic basement in the Bering Sea: U.S. Geological
    Survey map, in press.

Creager, J.S., Scholl, D.W., and others, 1973, Initial reports of the Deep Sea
    Drilling Project, v. 19: Washington, D.C., U.S. Govt. Printing Office,
    p. 193.

Davis, J.N., and House, L., 1979, Aleutian subduction zone seismicity,
    volcano-trench separation and their relation to great thrust-type
    earthquakes: Jour. Geophy. Research v. 84, p. 4583-4591.

DeLong, S.E., and McDowell, F.W., 1975, K-Ar ages from the Near Islands,
    western Aleutian Island, Alaska; Indication of a mid-Oligocene thermal
    event: Geology, v. 3, p. 691-694.

Drewes, H., Fraser, G.D., Snyder, G.L., Barnett, H.F., Jr., 1961; Geology of
    Unalaska Island and adjacent insular shelf, Aleutian Islands, Alaska:
    U.S. Geol. Survey Bull. 1028-S, p. 583-676.

Erickson, A., 1973, Initial report on downhole temperature and shipboard

thermal conductivity, measurements, Leg 19., Deep Sea Drilling Project,
in Creager, J.S., ed., and others, Initial reports of the Deep Sea
Drilling Project, v. 19: Washington, D.C., U.S. Govt. Printing Office,
p. 643-656.

Gardner, J.V., and Vallier, T.L., 1977a, Underway Geophysical Data Collected
on USGS Cruise S4-76, Southern Beringian Shelf: U.S. Geological Survey
Open File Report, OF77-524.

Gardner, J.S., and Vallier, T.L., 1977b, Map Showing Types and Distribution of
Faults Interpreted from Seismic Profiles in the St. George Basin Region,
Southern Bering Sea: U.S. Geological Survey Open File Report OF77-591.

Gardner, J.V., and Vallier, T.L., 1978, Underway Seismic Data Collected on
USGS Cruise S677, Southeastern Bering Sea: U.S. Geological Survey Open
File Report OF78-322.

Gates, O., G.D. Fraser, and G.L. Snyder, 1954, Preliminary report on the
geology of the Aleutian Islands: Science, v. 119, p. 446-447.

Gates, O., H.A. Powers, and R.E. Wilcox, 1971, Geology of the Near Islands,
Alaska: U.S. Geol. Survey Bull. 1028-U, p.709-822.

Grow, J.A., 1973, Crustal and Upper Mantle Structure of the Central American
Arc: Geo. Soc. Am. Bull., v. 84, p. 2169-2192.

Hein,, J.R., Scholl, D.W., Barron, J.A., Jones, M.G., and Miller, J., 1978,
Diagenesis of late Cenozoic diatomaceous deposits and formation of the
bottom simulating reflector in the southern Bering Sea: Sedimentology,
v. 25, p. 155-181.

Hopkins, D.M., and others, 1969, Cretaceous, Tertiary, and early Pleistocene
rocks from the continental margin in the Bering Sea: Geol. Soc. America
Bull., v. 80, p. 1471-1480.

Lee, H.J., 1973, Measurements and estimates of engineering and other physical

properties, Leg 19, in Creager, J.S., ed., and others, Initial reports of
the Deep Sea Frilling Project, v. 19: Washington, D.C., U.S. Govt.
Printing Office, p. 701-719.

Ludwig, W.J., S. Marauchi, N. Den, M. Ewing, H. Hotta, R.E. Houtz, T. Yoshii,
T. Asanuma, K. Hagiwara, T. Sato, and S. Ando, 1971, Structure of Bowers
Ridge, Bering Sea: Jour. Geophys. Research, v. 76, p. 6350-6366.

Marlow, M.S., Scholl, D.W., Buffington, E.C., Boyce, R.E., Alpha, T.R., Smith,
P.B., and Shipek, C.J., 1970, Buldir depressionte - Tertiary graben on
the Aleutian Ridge, Alaska: Marine Geology, v. 8, p. 85-108.

Marlow, M.S., Scholl, D.W., Buffington, E.C., and Alpha, T.R., 1973, Tectonic
history of the western Aleutian arc: Geol. Soc. America Bull., v. 84, p.
1555-1574.

Marlow, M.S., Scholl, D.W., Cooper, A.K., and Buffington, E.C., 1976,
Structure and evolution of Bering Sea shelf south of St. Lawrence
Island: Am. Assoc. Petroleum Geologists Bull., v. 60, p. 161-183.

Marlow, M.S., Cooper, A.K., Scholl, D.W., Alpha, T.R., 1976, Twenty-four
channel seismic reflection data acquired on the R/V S.P. LEE in Bering
Sea, 1975, and structure contours of acoustic basement beneath the
southern Bering Sea Shelf: U.S. Geological Survey Open File Report OF76-
652.

Marlow, M.S., Scholl, D.W., and Cooper, A.K., 1977, St. George basin, Bering
Sea shelf: a collapsed Mesozoic margin, in Island Arcs, Deep Sea
Trenches, and Back-Arc Basins, Maurice Ewing series: Amer. Geophysical
Union, v. 1, p. 211-220.

Marlow, M.S., Gardner, J.V., Vallier, T.L., McLean, H. Scott, E.W., and
Wilson, C.L., 1979a, Resource Report for Proposed OCS Lease Sale No. 70,
St. George Basin, Alaska: U.S. Geological Survey Open File Report, in

press.

Marlow, M.S., Cooper, A.K., Scholl, D.W., Vallier, T.L., and McLean, H.,
    1979b, Description of Dredge Samples from the Bering Sea Continental
    Margin: U.S. Geological Survey Open File Report, OF79-1139.

Miller, T.P., and Barnes, I., 1976, Potential for geothermal-energy
    development in Alaska--Summary; in Circum-Pacific Energy and Mineral
    Resources: Amer. Assoc. Petroleum Geologists Mem. 25, p. 151-154.

Miller, T.P., and Smith, R.L., 1977, Spectacular mobility of ash flows around
    Aniakchak and Fisher Calderas, Alaska: Geology, v. 5, p. 173-176.

Nichols, H., and R.B. Perry, 1966, Bathymetry of the Aleutian arc, Alaska:
    scale 1:400,000, 6 maps: U.S. Dept. Commerce, Environmental Sci.
    Services Admin., U.S. Coast and Geodetic Survey, Monograph 3.

Oil and Gas Journal, Sept. 3, 1979, p. 51.

Powers, H.A., R.R. Coast, and W. H. Nelson, 1960, Geology and submarine
    physiography of Amchitka Island, Alaska: U.S. Geol. Survey Bull. 1028-P,
    p. 521-554.

Robinson, G.D., 1947, Objectives, methods, and progress of Alaskan volcano
    investigations of the United States Geological Survey: U.S. Geological
    Survey Alaskan Volcano Investigations, Rept. no. 2, Progress of
    Investigations in 1946, p. 3-5.

Schlanger, S.O., and Combs, J., 1975, Hydrocarbon potential of marginal basins
    bounded by an island arc: Geology, July, p. 397-400.

Scholl, D.W., and Hopkins, D.M., 1967, Bering Sea shelf seismic reflection
    records, R/V THOMAS G. THOMPSON, U.S. Geological Survey Open File Report,
    OF68-238.

Scholl, D.W., Buffington, E.C., and Hopkins, D.M., 1968, Geologic history of
    the continental margin of North America in Bering Sea: Marine Geology,

v. 6, p. 297-330.

Scholl, D.W., and Hopkins, D.M., 1969, Newly discovered Cenozoic basins,
     Bering shelf: Alaska Amer. Assoc. Petroleum Geologists, Bull., v. 53, p.
     2067-2078.

Scholl, D.W., and others, 1969, Bering Sea seismic reflection profiles, U.S.
     Geological Survey Open File Report, OF70-292.

Scholl, D.W., Buffington, E.C., Hopkins, D.M., and Alpha, T.R., 1970, The
     Structure and Origin of the large Submarine Canyons of the Bering Sea:
     Marine Geol. 8, p. 187-210.

Scholl, D.W., H. G. Greene, and M.S. Marlow, 1970, Eocene age of Adak
     "Paleozoic(?)" rocks, Aleutian Islands, Alaska: Geol. Soc. America
     Bull., v. 81, p. 3582-3592.

Scholl, D.W., and Marlow, M.S., 1970, Diapirlike Structures in the
     Southeastern Bering Sea: Am. Assoc. Pet. Geol. Bull., Vol. 54, No. 9, p.
     1644-1650.

Scholl, D.W., and J.S. Creager, 1973, Geologic synthesis of Leg 19 (DSDP)
     results; far north Pacific, and Aleutian Ridge, and Bering Sea, in
     Initial Reports of the Deep Sea Drilling Project, v. 19: Washington,
     D.C., U.S. Government Printing Office, p. 897-913.

Scholl, D. W., E.C. Buffington, and M.S. Marlow, 1975a, Plate tectonics and
     the structural evolution of the Aleutian-Bering Sea region, in The
     geophysics and geology of the Bering Sea region: Geol. Soc. America Spec
     Paper 151, p. 1-31.

Scholl, D.W., Marlow, M.S., and Buffington, E.C., 1975b, Summit basins of
     Aleutian Ridge, North Pacific: Amer. Assoc. Petroleum Geologists Bull.,
     v. 59, p. 799-816.

Scholl, D.W., Buffington, E.C., Marlow, M.S., 1976, Aleutian-Bering Sea region seismic profiles U.S. Geological Survey Open File Report OF76-748.

Shepard, F.P., and Dill, R.F., 1966, Submarine canyons and other sea
valleys: Rand McNally & Company, Chicago, p. 381.

Shor, G.G., Jr., 1964, Structure of the Bering Sea and the Aleutian Ridge:
Marine Geology, v. 1, p. 213-219.

Sykes, L.R., 1971, Aftershock zones of great earthquakes, seismicity gaps, and
earthquake prediction for Alaska and the Aleutians: Jour. Geophys.
Research, v. 76,. p. 8021-8041.

Underwood, M.B., Vallier, T.L., Gardner, J.V., and Barron, J.A., 1979, Age,
grain size, mineralogy, and carbon/carbonate content of Miocene and
Pliocene samples from dredge hauls, DSDP holes 184b and 185, and the
Sandy River Well, southern Bering Sea continental margin and Alaska
Peninsula: U.S. Geol. Survey Open File Rept. OF79-450.

Vallier, T.L., Underwood, M.B., Gardner, J.V., and Barron, J.A., 1979, Neogene
Sedimentation on the Outer Continental Margin, Southern Bering Sea:
Marine Geol., in press.

Vallier, T.L., Underwood, M.B., Jones, D.L. and Gardner, J.V., 1979, Upper
Jurassic rocks from the continental shelf, southern Bering Sea: Amer.
Assoc. Petrol. Bull, in press.

Watanabe, T., Langseth, M.G., and Anderson, R.N., 1977, Heat flow in back-arc
basins of the western Pacific, in Island arcs, deep sea trenches, and
back-arc basins: v. 1, Am. Geophys. Union, p. 137-162.

Watts, A.B., 1975, Gravity field of the northwest Pacific ocean basin and its
margin - Aleutian Island Arc - Trench system, Geological Society of
America Map-Chart Series MC-10.

Wilcox, R.E., 1959, Igneous rocks of the Near Islands, Aleutian
Islands,Alaska, in Petrologia et mineralogia: 20th Internat. Geo. Cong.,
Mexico, D.F., sec. 11A, p. 365-378.

CPSIA information can be obtained
at www.ICGtesting.com
Printed in the USA
BVOW03s1012150317
478597BV00007B/66/P

9 781288 944545